# WITCHERY

# WITCHERY

## Embrace the
## Witch Within

Juliet Diaz

**HAY HOUSE**

Carlsbad, California • New York City
London • Sydney • New Delhi

**Published in the United Kingdom by:**
Hay House UK Ltd, The Sixth Floor, Watson House,
54 Baker Street, London W1U 7BU
Phone: +44 (0)20 3927 7290 · Fax: +44 (0)20 3927 7291; www.hayhouse.co.uk

**Published in the United States of America by:**
Hay House Inc., PO Box 5100, Carlsbad, CA 92018-5100
Tel: (1) 760 431 7695 or (800) 654 5126; Fax: (1) 760 431 6948 or (800) 650 5115
www.hayhouse.com

**Published in Australia by:**
Hay House Australia Ltd, 18/36 Ralph St, Alexandria NSW 2015
Tel: (61) 2 9669 4299; Fax: (61) 2 9669 4144; www.hayhouse.com.au

**Published in India by:**
Hay House Publishers India, Muskaan Complex, Plot No.3, B-2,
Vasant Kunj, New Delhi 110 070
Tel: (91) 11 4176 1620; Fax: (91) 11 4176 1630; www.hayhouse.co.in

A catalogue record for this book is available from the British Library.

Tradepaper ISBN: 978-1-78817-204-2
E-book ISBN: 978-1-78817-225-7

20  19  18  17  16  15  14  13  12  11

Interior images: 83 123RF/Artemii Sanin; 88 Shutterstock/Artur Balytskyi;
all other images 123RF/natashapankina

Printed in the United States of America

To my partner, Will Colón.
Thank you for being my protector, my wolf, and
for standing by me through the unraveling.

To my children, Aidan and Myka.
Thank you for being the best blessings. You have
changed my life in the most Magickal ways.

To my ancestors and guides.
Thank you for walking alongside me and
for guiding my every breath.

BEING A WITCH IS AN EMBODIMENT OF
YOUR TRUTH IN ALL ITS POWER.

# CONTENTS

# LIST OF RITUALS, SPELLS, POTIONS, AND PRACTICES

### Rituals

### Spells

### *Potions*

### *Practices*

### *The Witch's Garden of Herbal Magick*

#### ATTRACTING LOVE

## HEALING A BROKEN HEART

## PROTECTION

## SUCCESS

## WEALTH AND ABUNDANCE

## LUCK

# Beginning
## Your Journey

Being a Witch isn't about the hocus-pocus. And it isn't about what you buy, wear, or post on social media, or how you act. Being a Witch gives you the power to heal yourself, change your life, change the world, and conjure your every dream. In this book I will guide you on your journey to becoming a Witch and help you to connect with the Magick that lives within you. I explain how to cast off what doesn't serve you, how to unleash your authentic self, and how to become an embodiment of your truth. You'll also learn the skills and techniques needed when creating real Magick.

I'm Cuban with indigenous roots and come from a long line of Witch Healers. We believe in healing the mind, body, and spirit using the Earth's medicine along with spiritual guidance from our ancestors.

But you don't have to be born into a family of Witches, or initiated in a secret ritual, to be a Witch. There are hundreds of ways of being one. I was taught that we should each build our own personal form of Magickal craft, using the ancient ways but molding them so they feel just right for us. This is when our Magick is at its most powerful. My own Magick is a unique blend of practices, experiences, and teachings that I have brought together in a harmonious way that suits me. The importance of building and using a craft that is unique to me is one of the most vital lessons I have learnt in my life, and one I will pass on to you.

More of us than ever are feeling the fire of our inner Witch raging within, but there is an even greater reason to our calling than finding truth and self-acceptance, a greater reason why we feel the Earth bubbling beneath our feet: the Earth, our Mother, needs us! As Witches, the connection we have with the Earth allows us to feed back to her the Magickal energy we borrow, but there is much more to do in this day and age, when the Earth is ravaged by human behavior. By beckoning the Witch within to rise from the depths of your soul, you too can bring Magick to our Earth and help keep her healthy — and alive.

Even though I had a practicing family, I had to make my own decision to be a Witch. I had to realize my truth and make the decision to live within its unraveling — I like to believe that Witches are known for flying because they're not afraid to dive within. Remember that those who don't see your light are clouded by their own darkness. You were meant to rise, dear Witches! All beings are children of the Earth; we all come from the same cauldron. The power you hold was seeded in you long before your flesh tasted the air. You don't need to look outside yourself to seek acknowledgment — validation lives inside you.

It's taken me years of practice and experience to get where I am now, to become a fully embodied Witch in all her brilliance. But you, too, can step up to your calling, own your truth, and light up the world with your Magick!

It's time to embrace the Witch within.

 ## Ritual for anointing this book

This book is filled with wisdom, Magick, and love, ready for you to use on your journey. By anointing this book you will be able to connect with it in a deep, spiritual way, and in return it will provide more wisdom than you ever thought possible. Anointing the book will also activate the spell hidden within its pages which will help to magnify your connection and act as a guide.

## What you need

Dried mugwort, either loose or in a herb bundle; or incense — preferably frankincense, myrrh, or palo santo

A small bowl

A handful of rice

1 pinch salt

A white candle with a safe candleholder (a small taper candle is good for a relatively short spell like this one)

1 cup (250ml) water

## What to do

◊ Before any Magickal workings you need to cleanse your surrounding space, yourself, and your tools of any negative energies. This is done with the smoke of incense, resin, or dried herbs (loose or in a herb bundle). My favorites for cleansing include mugwort, rue, rosemary, palo santo, frankincense, myrrh, amber, and copal; however, some spells use specific herbs, resin, or incense for cleansing.

◊ Use matches to light incense or herb bundles (and candles, when using), then blow out any flames so they burn just enough to produce a light smoke. There are various ways to burn resins and loose herbs, but among the most common is to place a small amount on a charcoal disc. Leave the incense, resin, or herbs to burn near to where you're working or, for more extensive cleansing, carry them around your surrounding space, even through other rooms. Extinguish the incense or leave it burning for the remainder of your Magickal working or until it burns out.

◊ To anoint this book, after cleansing start the ritual by sitting in a quiet space and placing the book against your chest, next to your heart. Close your eyes, take three deep breaths, and try to clear your mind. Try to feel the book's subtle energies intertwine with yours. When you feel this connection, put the book down.

◊ Take the rice in your hand and bring it up to your lips. Blow at the rice very slowly for a count of three. Envision your breath turning the rice a golden color. Now place the rice in the bowl. Add the salt to the rice while saying the words 'A pinch of salt will do no harm. Instead it will bless a charm.'

◊ Take the book and place it in front of you. Light the candle and hold it in your right hand. Move the candle around the book counterclockwise three times while saying, 'With this flame I grant you into my journey. Guide me, guide me, guide me.' Blow out the candle and take a handful of the rice. Sprinkle it over the book while saying, 'I anoint you, I anoint you, I anoint you.' You can save the candle for another Magickal working if you wish.

◊ Dip your fingers into the water and draw a circle on your chest, by your heart, and say, 'I am ready to embrace my inner Witch.'

◊ You're now bound to Magick and to a commitment to continue your Magickal journey with clarity and focus.

PART ONE

# ROOT WORK

# WHAT IS MAGICK?

Magick is very real: it does exist. My confidence and belief in Magick are the reasons it's abundant within and all around me. Magick is also very alive within and all around you — you might just need to turn up the power a little. Even if you've never believed before, Magick is still there; it never goes away. It's a part of you. It's who you are.

Every entity in our world — the ocean, the trees, the mountains, animals, and people — is just one aspect of reality. Most are used to the physical workings of our presence here — what we see, feel, and hear. However, we miss the mark on what's beyond our physical perceptions: energy, spirits, ghosts. We're all an embodiment of energy, of power. Everything we do sends a command, created from our intent, into the collective web we weave, the single reality which together we all mold. This is how we create Magick — and make Magick work for us.

I want you to take a moment to think about what Magick means to you. Never mind definitions made by others; its presence should be unique to you, its meaning and feeling one that only you can explain — with your own heart and from your own experience. Everyone feels it differently and this is why it's so important that you start to pay close attention to self. We have become so programmed to find answers outside of ourselves that we end up feeling confused, disconnected, and lonely. Remember that you're Magick, and this has shown up before, even if you don't remember it. Once you start to reconnect with who you are and acknowledge that power within, your Magick will show up every day.

For me, Magick is unconditional love. It's shown up for me whenever I've needed it most. I suffered a childhood of poverty, fear, and abuse. The only memories of this time that are dear to me are the ones where Magick was present. I remember the first time I experienced Magick. I was sitting on the kitchen table, my pale and dirty bare legs hanging over the edge. I was two years old and my throat was so sore I could barely bring myself to speak. My mother was deep in the realm of her best Magick. Kitchen Witchery was her enchanting gift. I've never seen her more beautiful than when she was in the kitchen with her plants and herbs, giant pots over burning flames. The lace curtains were dancing in the wind and the smells of basil, lemon, and cilantro were swirling through my hair, her hips swaying to the sounds of the drums playing on the radio.

She is making soup for me, her own recipe. The smells are enchanting my being even before I have tasted the healing waters. Here she comes with a spoonful. I feel the Magick beaming from within the steam rising over the spoon, her love for me escaping her lips as she blows the heat away for me. *'Mmmmmm. Delicious, Mama.'* *'Not too salty?'* *'No, Mama.'*

To this day, my mother's Magick is at its best in the kitchen. She still blows the spoon just before she makes me taste something and asks me the same question. I want to tell her it's never over-salted, that she doesn't need to ask anymore, but then I'm reminded of how Magick can appear anywhere and in the subtlest of ways; that Magick is present every time my mother blows her love. If that's how it shows up, I should accept that and welcome it. We must all pay attention to these delicate moments in life that are so often overcast by harsh realities. Accept them as Magick showing up when you need it and giving you a warm embrace.

Magick isn't always about wielding power and manifesting your desires (though we will cover this sort of Magick later in the book). You need to learn to recognize it in all its different shades and realize that it exists in every detail of life. Magick is a walk in the woods and greeting the rays of sunshine pushing through the treetops. It's my youngest son's little fingers intertwined with mine when we walk to the car before I take him to school, and my older boy's beaming eyes as he tells me stories from his day. It's the soft kiss my husband places on my forehead before he leaves for work. Magick is experiencing pain, brokenness, and difficulty yet somehow seeing the light in that darkness.

MAGICK IS UNIQUE TO YOUR PRESENCE. IT IS YOUR OWN — A LOVE AFFAIR THAT IS WICKEDLY SACRED IN ALL WAYS.

Be mindful of your life; take notice of the Magick flowing through it. Learn to be still, to observe with all your senses. Notice those moments that make you feel something, the moments that stop you in your tracks, even if it's just for a second.

For instance, while writing this a delicious wind reached for my flesh, transporting me to another realm. My mind quieted and I stopped writing immediately to give it my full attention — my full being — as my body indulged in an act of passion between Magick and self. I acknowledged the Magick and it will continue to make love to me in all the ways it can. Have you ever made love to your very presence? To the sounds of the night or the warmth of the Sun? To the soft voices in the winds or to roaring thunder? Actually you have, though you may not have noticed it yet. It's our innate gift to connect to all things in this way. Making love isn't purely physical; it's an act of spirit so powerful that it floods the gates of our flesh. It's connection.

CONNECTION FEELS ORGASMIC
WHEN YOU ALLOW YOURSELF
TO WONDER IN STILLNESS.

Record these moments, write them down, and explain exactly what you felt. With time, they'll become much more powerful and come around more frequently. Believe me, if you're experiencing them in this way, you'll want them to come as often as possible. All it takes is for you to notice.

# THE POWER OF
# A MAGICKAL
# ATTITUDE

'A Magickal attitude' is what I call the characteristics of one's energy, or vibe. These characteristics influence everything that happens, or doesn't happen, in our lives. Your Magickal attitude affects what your Magick can manifest, and without this understanding you'll never bring to fruition what you desire. Your spells, intentions, and rituals won't be fully effective – they may not even work at all.

Even the attitude toward self is crucial. How we think and feel about ourselves directly impacts our Magick and its ability to manifest what we want. Think of yourself as a paper package. The look and feel of the wrapping paper is affected by everything inside this package, both spiritually and physically. Our goal is to unwrap this package, one layer at a time, until we get to what's inside — the core, the center, the seed, the spirit. The force.

The Law of Attraction states that positivity manifests positivity and negativity manifests negativity, and the same applies when working with Magick. I have noticed one key factor in my students' struggle to manifest their spells and intentions, and that is that they all have expectations. But setting expectations sets limits, and when you set limits you're telling your Magick that you're limited, so it will only respond with limitations. You must see the potential in all and believe that anything is possible. Your Magickal attitude is extremely important in helping you experience your best Magickal life.

Having a Magickal attitude asks that you:

### *Take responsibility for your actions*

It's important for you to start owning up to your actions. Blaming other people, situations, or experiences for your actions is no excuse and will not help you to manifest a Magickal attitude. So from now on remember that you have a choice in everything you say and do.

### *Surround yourself with positive people*

Connect only with those who are supportive, who inspire you, and who celebrate your accomplishments. Banish those who are filled with negativity, greed, and jealousy.

Don't waste your precious time on Earth with those who choose to drown in their pessimism — you'll go down with them.

## Check yourself

Be mindful of your own attitude and vibe. Know when to step back and adjust your presence, your self; to take a moment to realign with your truth, your purpose; to bring yourself back to your body; and to raise your frequency, cutting out negativity, and reaching a higher state of consciousness.

## Stay positive

Master your own thoughts and learn to escape traps of the mind. Always see the good in things and try to focus on the best outcome of any situation. Know that overdramatizing can lead you straight into fear. Try to stay in the middle ground, without expectations.

## Remember: shit happens

When things you do go wrong, remind yourself how far you've gotten and how proud you are of yourself. Just allow the shit to fall and gracefully clean it up afterward. Remember that you are your worst critic; it's you who feeds negativity within, so start feeding the soul instead.

### Set realistic goals

Manifesting your intents has no limits, but start with achievable, realistic goals and prioritize those that matter most in your life right now.

### Address everyday issues

Face any issues that mess with your vibe and handle them productively. If you need to take a moment before you do this, take it; nothing is ever healed with rage. Allow your initial emotions to pass, then go back to the issue with a calm heart and clear mind.

### Know that things are rarely that serious

Stop sweating the small stuff or turning tiny monsters into beasts. Keep your emotions from taking over.

### See your life as a blessing

Focus on what you have, what is already present, and on what really matters. Don't trap yourself in wanting what you don't or can't have. Practice gratitude.

### Believe in yourself

You're stronger than you think and more powerful than you believe. Be your No. 1 fan and cheer yourself on. You can do this! You are Magick!

### Compare only with yourself

Your journey is yours alone. Others' accomplishments and wins are not your losses. Instead get inspired to find yourself and what works for you. Focus on the way you want to live, rather than judging others for the way they live. See a pattern here? The only one you should be looking at is you.

### Be yourself

Stay true to yourself. If you don't know what that looks like, start by saying No and cutting out the things in your life that don't resonate with you. Fill your life with what makes you happy and what really resonates with you. Don't think about what you *should* look or how you *should* act; you're unique.

### Protect your vibe

Keep as far away as possible from Energy Vampires – people who suck the Magick out of you. Most don't even know they're doing it, but you have to stay aware. Always be mindful of your presence. If you start to feel off and things just don't seem right, if a person or thing doesn't make you feel good, stay away.

### *Allow yourself to feel*

We're often so busy we don't pay attention to what we're feeling, but if we ignore negative feelings they can pile up and leave us emotionally and physically drained. So each day, find time to sit quietly, close your eyes, and relax, then focus on your emotions. Are you tired? Are you stressed? Is there something that's secretly annoying you? Pay attention to these feelings and how you can work through them.

Your thoughts and feelings have the power to affect everything in and around you. There will be obstacles but you needn't take this as a sign of defeat; obstacles are signs from the cosmos, warning us that something is off-balance or not working. Their presence means you're already in the spirit of Magick and trying to manifest the world you want. So give yourself some slack.

There is a method to the madness of unraveling, and it can be downright agonizing. It takes practice and devotion, but soon you'll be able to call in abundance, wealth, healthy relationships, and anything else that your Witchy heart desires.

# Q&A FOR NEW WITCHES

If you think being a Witch is just about cooking up spells, you're mistaken. Yes, we practice Witchcraft, but most importantly we *become* it. It's like a second skin, so familiar that with every breath we mold the world around us.

There are other things a potential Witch might want to know, such as 'Is Witchcraft evil?' or 'What kind of Witches are there?' So here are the questions I'm asked most often, and that every would-be Witch should know the answers to before they even consider the world of Magick.

### Are there different types of Witch?

Yes, there are certain types or paths that some Witches choose to follow. However, it's gravely important that, if you choose one, you mold it to work for you. Look into various different crafts, philosophies, and practices, and add what connects with you to your own practice. Your practice will be forever changing, just as you change with the years. Nothing is ever set in stone. Flow like the waters, dear Witches.

## Can I believe what I read about Witchcraft?

Many books and articles about Witchcraft are based on personal opinion. For example, a lot of material is written by followers of Wicca and its content is influenced by the religion. The same goes for other paths, but reading an author's biography is usually a good indicator of their beliefs. Don't be discouraged if at first you don't connect to anything you read. Be patient, and keep studying and exploring.

## Can I continue with my religion?

Most of the thousands of students in my November Sage Herbarium - A Witch Healers' School, follow a religion or have done in the past. Among others I have Catholic Witches, Jewish Witches, and Witches from voodoo religion. It's okay to have a religion and practice Witchcraft at the same time, so try not to worry what others think – just do what feels right for you as long as you're not causing harm to anyone or anything.

## *How quickly can I become a Witch?*

Real Magick is nothing like the magic you see in *Harry Potter*, *Sabrina*, or *Charmed*. We can't just whip out a wand and have things magically happen in an instant (and you most definitely can't fly on a broom!). Results can take time – even with total devotion and constant practice it may be two or three months before your efforts pay off, though it's possible for small changes to appear within two or three weeks. However, sometimes nothing will happen at all (*see page 215*). I truly believe anyone can be a Witch, but just saying you're one doesn't make you one. You need to do the work and to live and breathe Magick every day. Be patient – and practice, practice, practice! And then practice some more!

## *Do I need a teacher?*

It's great to have a teacher who is willing to help you along your path, and even better if they allow you to witness firsthand how they work their Magick. However, avoid teachers who push their ways onto you or who make you feel uncomfortable or belittled. If you're not completely happy with your teacher, leave. And if you experience any sort of abuse, speak up. You don't deserve to be harmed, emotionally or physically. You're priceless, precious, and sacred.

### Will I need to wear special clothes?

There is no 'Witchy' style. What you might have in your head is made up by the media. I knew this from a very young age because each of the Witches in my family dressed differently from each other and, as I grew up, I discovered that every Witch was unique. I've met Witches who dress in Goth, florals, robes, Victorian dresses, and in jeans and T-shirts, biker jackets, Walmart, and Prada. And you don't need to wear black unless it's the color you want to wear anyway. You should wear whatever you like!

### What is the difference between Black Magick and White Magick?

Magick and Witchcraft aren't black or white, good or bad. They just *are*. What you do with this power is up to you. Yes, there are awful people out there using Magick to harm others, and involvement with these negative energies lowers your frequency, allowing ill-willed spirits into your life. Use your intuition; if someone or something feels wrong, don't engage — unfriend. Always protect yourself by staying away from negative people or situations; you can also carry protective herbs, crystals, and gems (*see page 161*).

### Will I need to worship the Devil?

Religions, the media, and the arts have often shown Witches as evil and dabbling in so-called Black Magick, misrepresenting Witches by showing them worshiping something demonic. But worshipping the Devil or Demons doesn't make you a Witch; what you worship or believe in is up to you. Worshipping a specific deity or Satan is not a 'Witch thing,' it's the choice of each individual.

### Are Witches always part of a coven?

Choosing whether or not to be in a coven – a group of Witches who meet regularly to perform Magick, rituals, and ceremonies – is a personal choice. Many covens have their own rules and beliefs, so you must first find yourself before following anyone else's path. But if you find a coven that you connect with, then sure – go for it! Covens in the modern world are very different from how they used to be and are more flexible about individuals' needs and experience.

You can always start your own coven! Ninety per cent of the time I practice alone, but I created a coven so I can enjoy the company of my fellow Witches. We don't always perform Magickal workings together – we go out to dinner, we go out hiking to worship the Earth, and we do a lot of work for charity. What matters about a coven is that it feels good and it feels right for you.

You'll discover answers to most of the other questions you might have about being a Witch later in the book, so read on.

# UNLEASH
# YOUR POWER

It's never too late to unleash your Magickal power. It lives within the Witch that's inside each and every one of us, whatever our color, race, gender, religion, career, opinions, or aesthetic — regardless of any one thing at all. A Witch is an embodiment of self that breathes fire through your spine. Embracing your inner Witch will unleash your Magickal power.

Unleashing your power starts the moment you believe you're powerful. Key to discovering your truth is understanding who you are and who you are not. You must be willing to dive into the depths, to shed all the layers of falsities, and to meet your unveiled self. You'll experience pain and discover brutal truths as you face the being behind the shadows, but also healing, self-love, and forgiveness. It's a beautifully painful, blessed unraveling, and once you discover that truth, your power can no longer be hidden or contained.

It hurts my soul knowing that Witches were once forced into a suppressed mindset in order to keep their power hidden. Our innate power was turned into something to fear, something to be ashamed of, and a mockery. We were beaten, tortured, and burnt. It's with grave importance that we take back our power and stop the friction between body and soul by lubricating ourselves with our Magick.

So don't keep your power hidden or imprisoned any longer. You're needed. You're important to the evolution of consciousness. And know that you're never alone – you'll always have ancestors who walk alongside you and guide you.

There are three vital steps to unleashing your Magickal power: let go of your ghosts, connect with our Mother, and live your most authentic life.

## Let go of your ghosts

We have each been scarred by emotions, events, and other situations. These scars haunt us like ghosts, each one sapping our light, dimming our Magickal power. They're all a burden to your potential. Hanging on to pain, resentment, anger, and fear will keep you from embodying your authentic self, your truth, in all its brilliance. So let go of those pieces of your past that don't serve you. Free yourself from your own haunting. Learn to accept who you are, as you are, and love yourself unapologetically.

## Bath spell for banishing the ghosts within

I have found this spell to be beneficial for major transitions, including the expulsion of ghosts from the past. It not only releases you from unwanted energies, but also blesses your new journey ahead. You can use this spell whenever you feel like you need alignment and clarity too. Perform it only when the lunar cycle has reached a Full Moon. The time of day is up to you.

### Step 1: Create a potion for banishing negative energy

#### What you need

- 1 cup (250ml) cold water
- 1 tablespoon honey
- 1 lemon slice
- 1 garlic clove, crushed
- 1 pinch salt
- 1 pinch dried basil or star anise powder, or 1 whole star anise
- 1 sprig rosemary
- 1 bay leaf

## What to do

◊ Add all the ingredients to the water and stir for 1–2 minutes.

### Step 2: Perform the spell

## What you need

For cleansing: dried herbs (choose from cedar, mugwort, rosemary, sweetgrass, or bay leaf), either loose or in a bundle; or incense (choose from palo santo, copal, frankincense, or myrrh)

For the bath: the potion you made in Step 1

An essential oil you find relaxing, such as lemon balm, hyssop, frankincense, bergamot, or lavender

2–3 handfuls fresh petals from any sort of flower

1 cup (300g) Himalayan or sea salt

½ cup (50g) one or two dried herbs – choose from rosemary, basil, fennel, or rue

A white candle

Crystals (optional) that help with release, such as smoky quartz, or that encourage love and healing, such as rose quartz

## What to do

◊ Use the smoke of your dried herbs or incense to cleanse the bathroom, your tools, and yourself.

◊ Fill the bath at your preferred temperature, then add the potion you made in Step 1, plus 4–6 drops of your chosen essential oil, the petals, the salt, and your chosen bath herbs. (I like to really pull out the herbs' properties by boiling them in water for about 10 minutes, then adding this infusion once cooled.)

◊ Place your candle and crystals around the bathtub, then dim or turn off the bathroom lights.

◊ Hold the candle, unlit, close to your chest, close your eyes, and take three deep breaths. Connect your energy to the candle. Feel the warmth from your hands enter the candle and envision an amber light in and around it. Then say the following: 'Amber light from within my soul, enter this candle and take hold. Release me from the things that have bound me to a self that isn't true. Leave me be as I am meant to be – light so bright, the self that's right.' Adapt these words if you like.

◊ Now place the candle somewhere in the bathroom, light it, and keep it burning until you've finished the spell.

◊ Kneel by the bathtub and thank the water for the healing it will bless you with, then say a gentle goodbye to your old self.

◊ Step into the bath and dwell in its healing waters for as long as you like. (If you have your period, don't worry – this will actually amplify the Magick, and you'll be showering at the end of the spell in any case.) Close your eyes, be still, and think of the things you want to let go until you feel them lift out of you. Face the emotions attached to each one and allow yourself to feel them, then release them. Don't hold back: if you feel the need to scream, go ahead – let it all go!

◊ Once you feel you've finished, drain the bath, retaining as many as possible of the herbs and flowers.

◊ Once the water has drained, take a cold shower for just a couple of minutes. Try not to stress about the cold – Witch up! You got this! As you wash your body, picture the water filling you with light.

◊ You need to hydrate and relax after a release like this so drink some water and take time out. Also, avoid using any technology.

◊ As soon as is convenient, discard the leftover herbs and flowers at a crossroads or anywhere facing east, preferably on dirt for Mother Earth to take away.

## Connect with our Mother

Earth is our Mother: she gives life and she nurtures. She is a womb from which we're all her children. Connecting with Mother Earth doesn't mean you have to love hiking or lounging among mosquitoes. It simply means connecting your energies with the Earth's. Knowing how each season affects you is vital to your Magickal power; you can even amplify your Magickal power by using the energies of the current season, other annual cycles and astrological events (*see page 95*). This is why the fragility of our Mother isn't to be taken lightly: Witches have a harmonious exchange with the Earth that feeds our Magick and gives it back to her, so we need to care for our Mother, be close to her, and never abuse her.

## Live your most authentic life

Living your most authentic life means living a life in which you show up as all that you are, with full control of your entire self. Think about it: who are you really? What do you like, love, and dislike? What makes you happy? What upsets you? What are your passions and dreams? Who is the true soul within the flesh? Have you met yourself unveiled? Only when you live and breathe your truth will you embody your true potential and greatest Magickal power. Living your truth doesn't mean you have to come out of the broom closet, however. You don't need to tell others what you do or practice, if you don't want to. Being a practicing Witch isn't about the show, it's about embracing the Witch within.

I believe we can live purposefully and fully by allowing our Magick to work for us. Take control of your life and weave it into whatever dreams you hold. Embrace your self and emotions without shame and make yourself a priority. Know that you're capable of changing the course of your own life, that you're infinitely Magickal and that nothing and no one can take that away from you.

### Ritual for reclaiming your Magickal power

This ritual aims to release you from anything that has taken your power, such as a painful experience, or anyone who has, such as a bully. In order to amplify your power you need to release what doesn't serve you and let it go.

Take your time with this ritual. Take a break if you want to, or stop the ritual completely – especially if you feel anything other than empowered by it or you find the ritual overwhelming.

It can be performed at any time and as many times as you like to bring you back to your power.

## What you need

Dried herbs — choose from rue, yerba santa, or cedar — either loose or in a bundle; or incense — choose from frankincense, myrrh, or palo santo

3 candles, preferably white

A small bowl of salt

A bowl of water

## What to do

◊ Find a quiet place to perform the ritual then cleanse the space and yourself with the dried herbs or incense. You can also burn these, or resin, to create a soothing environment. Sit on the floor or at a table and set one candle to your left, one to your right, and one directly in front of you. Light the candles then place the bowl of salt on the left, and the bowl of water on the right. Close your eyes for a moment, clear your mind, and take three deep breaths. Allow your body to relax and release all fears, worries, and noise from within. This is now your sacred space, full of light and comforting healing energies from Mother Earth. Allow her Elements — earth, air, fire, and water — to surround you and to envelop you with love.

◊ When you're ready, take a pinch of salt and sprinkle it into the water as you say aloud, or in your head, the name of the event, person, or situation from which you're reclaiming your Magickal power. For example, 'I reclaim my power from my friend [name], who constantly belittles me: "I take my power back from you."' Repeat these words as often as you need to until you feel release and a sense of calm comes over you.

◊ Now sit in stillness for a moment. Feel your energy vibrating with Magick and free of unnecessary weight. Blow out the candles from left to right then take the bowl of salty water and empty it into the Earth at the base of a tree, or in a river or stream that flows away from where you live, or at a crossroads.

Another method that works wonderfully in taking back your power, whether from those who have hurt you or from negative experiences you've inflicted upon yourself, is to write letters—though they're not for sending. Healing letters, as I call them, are for your own spiritual cleansing and will allow you to move forward in life. Not only has writing such letters helped me and hundreds of my clients, it's been proven to work in the healing process. The letter will allow you to forgive the ghosts living within and to let them go; you'll then be free of them.

##  Ritual for writing a healing letter

The point is to get all your raw emotions onto that paper to release everything that haunts you so you can take back your power. Proper grammar and spelling don't matter, and you don't need to reread or edit what you've written. This letter is for you and for your eyes only. Take a break if you need to, but stop if writing down your emotions and thoughts makes you feel worse, not better — this ritual may not be for you.

### What you need

A good supply of writing paper

A pen

### What to do

◊ Find a quiet space where you're free from distractions and interruptions. Write the name of the person or a short description of the situation that has hurt you; this can include yourself, for causing pain with self-neglect or addiction for instance. If you don't remember any names, make them up. Now start writing to this person or event — and don't hold back! Write whatever comes into your mind, even if it doesn't make sense. You might tell this person or event how they made you feel, or you might tell them something you've always wanted to say but haven't. For example, 'To Steven, what you did to me is unforgivable. You were supposed to care for me and instead you hurt me and created monsters in my life. I forgive you, so that I may free myself from you.'

◊ What you write is up to you. Allow yourself to cry and scream through your writing (but keep breathing deeply to help yourself stay focused). Releasing a ghost isn't easy; it can be agonizing. This is a time to be brutally honest about self.

◊ When you've finished writing, place your hand on the page you've finished. Now close your eyes, take a deep breath, and slowly count aloud to 20. With each count, feel the energy of the ghost rising from within then leaving you. Envision this energy as black smoke and watch it leave your body and disappear into the wind.

◊ Once you reach 20, take another deep breath and be still for a moment. Allow yourself to go through the emotions that rose up as you wrote the letter and be still until they calm. Repeat three times: 'I take back my power from you,' then open your eyes.

◊ Now put the pages together and fold them in half (do the same if you've used a single page). Lick your thumb and press it onto the top, or sole, page while saying, 'I vow to release you, ghost, and to never allow you back in. I will never give you my power.' Using a part of yourself – such as your saliva from licking your thumb — amplifies any Magickal workings. Instead of moistening my thumb by licking it, I choose to wet it with a drop of my menstrual blood; or you can spit into a cup of water, add a pinch of salt, and use that. Do whatever feels most comfortable for you.

◊ Stow the pages of your letter in this book or in a journal. Keeping them represents your choice to take back your power and adds to the positives manifesting in your life. Alternatively, you can choose to burn the letters as an act of banishing, then scatter the ashes onto the earth or into a stream or river.

# THE ART OF
# SELF-LOVE

*'Your task is not to seek love, but merely
to seek and find all the barriers within
yourself that you have built against it.'*

RUMI

It's through self-love that you learn to find and release anything hindering your inner Magick, and to appreciate, respect, and be grateful for every aspect of your self. It requires you to be compassionate and devote time to building a relationship with your self and finding your truth. In finding your truth you find your Magick. This is where we embrace the Witch within.

A Witch is only as powerful as the love she gives herself. Self-love is about making the decision to get your life together; it's about organizing your bills, saving money, eating more healthily, and working out; it's also about looking your emotions in the face; shedding toxic people, friends, and partners from your life; and switching off your phone and taking a break from the madness of the world. It's about being yourself and taking responsibility for everything you say and do.

Self-love isn't selfish. It isn't a free card to belittle others or to think you're better than them. It doesn't compare, judge, or compete. It's about making choices to better your own life ahead; a way to understand that you don't need to be fixed, but to be loved and cared for by the person who matters the most — you.

> UNVEIL, COME FORTH AS YOU ARE,
> DEAR WITCH. THE WORLD NEEDS
> YOU. MOTHER EARTH CALLS YOU.

Here is a list of practices to help you achieve self-love and to manage your life, not run from it — and they all help to amplify your inner Magick. You don't have to follow all of them; they're practices that I hope will inspire you to create your own.

### Make self-care essential

Self-care is the act of deliberately looking after your physical, spiritual, and emotional self so you're able to maintain a strong connection to your spirit and your

Magick. Your own self-care doesn't have be the same as anyone else's. Mine includes daily meditation, hot yoga, eating healthy foods, and creating Magick. Don't discount self-care that may seem odd to others. For instance, I also find that masturbating is self-care, as is time out from calls, texts, and social media.

## Tune in with a tiny ritual

I run two businesses, I'm a mother and I devote a lot of time to friends, family, the community, and activism, so throughout the day I practice tiny rituals of self-connection. They're moments to say to myself, 'Hey, I see you. Slow it down a little and realign.' My favorite tiny rituals include drinking tea and stretching. I also repeat positive affirmations, either in my head or out loud. Discover what tiny rituals work best for you.

## Pursue your passions

Who are we, if not what sets our heart on fire? There is no shame in pursuing your passions or living how you want to live. Of course, most of us have bills to pay and other responsibilities, so take it one step at a time, perhaps doing a side gig until you have enough momentum to change your situation. Not sure what your passions are? Try a new activity each week and notice what makes you vibe highest.

### Listen to the true you

Learn how to tell your true self from the voices of ghosts from your past. The voices of ghosts will usually lead you the wrong way, making you believe you're not good enough and holding you back from your authentic life. But your intuition will show you the right way, so learn how to recognize it – and the real you.

### High-five yourself

Write little notes of positivity and stick them around the house where you know you're going to see them. Write compliments, even, and reminders of how powerful you are. Everyday life can quickly get in the way of what's important to you and your purpose, so these little notes will help bring you back to self.

### Take time out, within

Meditate as often as possible. Through meditation one finds inner wisdom, peace, and connection – and it really turns up the volume on your Magick. You can even meditate while you're active, during yoga, swimming, hiking, knitting, and so on – anything that quiets mental noise and distractions and that makes you feel trance-like.

## *Hang out with nature*

Connecting to our Mother, Earth, is one of the best methods of self-love. She brings us back to our roots, balances and grounds us, releases body and spirit from negativity, and reminds us of who we are outside of the digital world. Walk on the grass barefoot, go on picnics, explore trails in the woods, lounge by lakes — just get outside and back to nature at least once a week.

## *Look after Mother Earth*

Doing things that help Mother Earth is where the heart of the Witch truly thrives. Focus on simple things that will fit into your day yet make a big difference, such as picking up garbage on your path, helping a lost animal, or watering thirsty plants. Cut down your consumption of meat and dairy, whose production uses a much greater percentage of agricultural resources than their nutritional worth deserves.

## *Say No to negativity*

One of the most important self-love practices is to protect yourself from negative vibes and energies (*see page 137*). Most of us are natural empaths — we feel what others feel, but that goes for negativity too. This can affect our mood, and if this happens too frequently it can affect our health too.

## *Put your house in order*

Organize your house, bills, and other tasks. Just get shit done, Witches. Set goals or make a to-do list for the day or week, then prioritize your tasks. When you know things are under control, or just that there's a plan, you'll alleviate any stress or worries. It's fine just to relax some days, but always remember that if you have big dreams there's work to be done to make them a reality.

## Spells to encourage self-love

We can all use a little encouragement from time to time, especially when it comes to giving attention to self and indulging in self-love. These spells all magnify the heart, turning it inward to self.

### Bath spell for coming back to self

This spell is perfect for those needing to balance, unwind, and clear negativity. It's like a hug for your energy.

#### What you need

I cup (250g) Epsom salts

I cup (300g) pink Himalayan salt

I orange, sliced

½ cup (25g) each of at least 3 of the following dried herbs and flowers: lavender, rose petals, jasmine, basil, lemon balm, calendula, or hyssop

1 lemon, sliced

3 drops of 1 or 2 essential oils — choose from bergamot, rose, or lavender

A white, pink, or red candle

Small bowl of any of the following crystals: carnelian, rose quartz, or smoky quartz

1 tablespoon cinnamon

Incense — choose from cedar, dragon's blood, palo santo, lavender, or rose

## What to do

◊ Fill the bath at your preferred temperature. Meanwhile bring a big saucepan of water to boil, add the salts, orange slices, and dried herbs or flowers, then simmer for five minutes.

◊ Add the contents of the saucepan to the bath, along with the lemon slices and essential oils. In a safe place in the bathroom, light the candle and position it next to the bowl of crystals.

◊ On a small piece of paper write a short description of what you want from this bath, such as focus, release, balance, and so on. Place the note in the bowl of crystals and sprinkle some cinnamon over it.

◊   Light the incense and move it around your body to allow the smoke to cleanse you. Leave the incense burning during your bath. You may play some soothing music as well, if you like.

◊   As you bathe, keep in mind the desire on your note. Using a cup or your hands, pour the bath water around your neck and shoulders, and over and around your head. The spell is complete.

◊   Dispose of the note, but you may reuse the bowl of crystals and the candle when you next perform this spell.

*Foot-soak spell for recharging and resetting*

A foot-soak spell draws any impurities and stagnant energy you may be harboring down through the feet and into the water, and gives you a reset. This spell is particularly good for those who feel they're stuck in their lives and not going anywhere. It charges you with positive and protective energies, and opens opportunities in your life, allowing abundance to flow in.

## What you need

Footbath or similar container in which you can comfortably fit both feet

4–7 drops of 1 or 2 essential oils — choose from cedar, eucalyptus, geranium, or rosemary

1 cup (120g) oats

1 cup (250ml) milk (dairy or nut)

½ cup (125g) sea salt

½ cup (125g) Epsom salts

3 tablespoons ground coffee

½ cup (180g) honey

1 cup (50g) mixed dried rosemary, sage, basil, and calendula

Incense or scented candle — choose from cedar, sandalwood, juniper, or lavender

## What to do

◊ Fill the footbath with warm water at a temperature you find comfortable. Add the essential oil, oats, milk, salts, coffee, honey, and herbs. Light the incense or candle.

◊ Soak your feet for a minimum of 20 minutes, allowing the mixture to do its work. This is a silent spell so there must be no distractions, not even music. Try to close your eyes and meditate.

◊ Once you've soaked your feet, wash them with cold water. Dispose of the spell water in dirt at the base of a tree, in a river that flows away from where you live, or at a crossroads.

## Honey jar spell for deep reflection

I usually use honey jar spells for matters of love and wealth, but this is one I have tweaked to amplify your love for self. It will also bring deep healing and protect you from anything that may disrupt your love for self. Its effects will continue throughout your life.

### What you need

Rosemary herb bundle; or incense – choose from dragon's blood, copal, or star anise

Small piece of torn brown parcel paper and a pen

Full jar of honey and a teaspoon

1 pinch each of lovage root, dried basil, and dried rose petals

A strand of your hair, a clipping from one of your nails, or a drop of your menstrual blood

Enough salt to sprinkle in a circle around the jar

1 cinnamon stick

1 sprig rosemary

2–3 cloves

1 small rose quartz

Cinnamon essential oil – enough to dip your fingers into

A small red or white taper candle

## What to do

◊ Cleanse your space with the dried herbs or incense, then lay out next to you everything you'll need. On the brown paper draw a personal symbol of love and write a short intent, such as 'I love myself unconditionally,' 'I deserve and am worthy of love,' or simply 'self-love.'

◊ Open the jar and eat a teaspoon of honey, then slowly and passionately recite the intention you wrote, either out loud or in your head. Repeat twice, each time eating another teaspoon of honey.

◊ Place the brown paper in front of you and in the center of it put a pinch each of the lovage root, basil, and rose petals. Add your hair, nail clipping, or menstrual blood. Fold the furthest side of the paper toward you, then continue folding the paper until it's as small as possible. Put the paper into the jar and gently push it into the honey with the spoon. Sprinkle the salt counterclockwise around the jar. Take the cinnamon stick, rosemary, cloves, and rose quartz and put them in the jar as well, then screw the lid onto the jar.

◊ Now anoint your candle by dipping your finger into the cinnamon oil and smoothing the oil onto the candle in a downward motion from top to bottom. Light the candle and drip a little of the wax onto the lid of the jar so you can fix the burning candle onto the lid. Now let the candle melt all over the lid and sides of the jar until it's sealed. (This isn't meant to look pretty or perfect.)

◊ Once the candle has burnt out and the wax has set hard, place the jar either on your altar (*see page 123*) or under the side of the bed you sleep on. Alternatively, bury it in a hole in the dirt, backfilling it halfway, and planting any flower or herb seed before filling the hole completely. Water the seed and sit by it for a moment while you ask that our Mother take this spell and make it grow.

## Mirror spell for reflecting healing energy

This spell is great not only for igniting powerful love within and for banishing stress and anxiety, but also for spreading healing energies out into the world.

### What you need

A mirror on a table

A glass of cold water

A silver-colored candle

Cinnamon oil

1 teaspoon dried basil

1 teaspoon dried rose petals

A small clear quartz crystal

### What to do

◊ Think of a self-love affirmation you want to give yourself — for example, 'I love myself because I am worthy of love.' Sit comfortably facing the mirror. Place the glass of water and the candle directly in front of you then light the candle. Put three drops of cinnamon oil into the water, followed by the basil and the rose petals. Place the quartz in the water too.

◊ Gaze at the candle flame for a moment while you focus on relaxing and clear your mind. When you're ready, look into the mirror and gaze into your eyes. In a chant-like manner, recite your affirmation over and over, each time feeling your energy vibrating more and more strongly within.

◊ Picture a bright pink light radiating within and around your body, pulsing and growing until it pushes out into the universe. Keep going until you feel like you've washed away all negative thoughts or energies.

◊ Tell yourself how grateful you are for having done this spell for yourself. Now blow out the candle.

◊ Keep the glass, which is now filled with your healing and loving energy, on your altar, by your bed, or anywhere you prefer; it will continue to fill your space with love and healing energies. Throw away the contents after three days.

PART TWO

# THE CRAFT
# UNVEILED

# BEGINNING YOUR MAGICKAL PRACTICE

There are a great many techniques and skills required for different Magickal practices, but I'm going to share with you some of the most fundamental. You may find that you learn some techniques more quickly than others – this is perfectly normal, just take your time with each one. If you find you want to tweak the way you learn them, do so. The methods I share are a starting point for you to build your own Magickal craft. A true Witch is a practicing Witch, and our craft is constantly evolving. Even when we think we have mastered a skill, we continue to find ways to amplify it.

It may not always be clear why some of the techniques are important, but believe me when I tell you they're all meant to aid particular aspects of spell-casting and

Witchcraft. For instance, you need to know how to clear the mind and focus on your intent; how to raise your energy to enhance your Magickal workings; and how to harness power from the Elements and how to use it. With dedicated practice you'll begin to experience the true power of your Magick.

# MEDITATION

In order for your Magick to reach its full potential you need to be able to banish all external distractions and come to a place of stillness, both mentally and physically, so you can focus on what you're trying to wield. Meditation does just that — it clears the mind of anything that can interfere with your energy and enhances your Magick by raising your consciousness and self-awareness. It's also a powerful way of bringing positive energy into your presence and expanding your capacity for manifestation.

Every Witch should meditate daily, in the way they choose, to strengthen the communication between mind, body, and spirit. Practice until you can close yourself off from distractions wherever you are, allowing yourself to meditate anytime, anywhere.

## Meditation practices

There's no right or wrong way to meditate. However, it's good to start with the basics and so in the following pages I'll give you four techniques to try. Find the one that speaks to you the most.

Essential oils, incense, crystals and gems, and herbs and teas are commonly used to enhance the experience of meditation. Here are the ones that work best for me in meditation, with a guide to using them.

### Herbs

Fennel, calendula, hibiscus, chamomile, lavender, lemongrass, nettle

A bundle of whole dried herbs can be gently burnt for its smoke, or you can place it on a charcoal disc that should be lit until it's white hot.

You can also steep fresh or dried herbs in freshly boiled water to make a tea to drink before meditating.

### Incense

Sandalwood, lavender, lemongrass, pine, amber, cinnamon

Light incense so that the smoke fills your space with its Magickal scent, or use a charcoal disc with herbs (*as above*).

### Essential oils

Frankincense, myrrh, cedar, lavender, palo santo, sage, mugwort

Use the oils in a diffuser, or dilute them in a base oil and dab onto your skin.

### Crystals and gems

Apophyllite, azurite, celestite, amethyst, quartz, danburite, selenite

Place the crystals or gems around you or wear them in some way.

 ## Deep meditation using crystal energy

Focusing on your breathing is one of the simplest and oldest forms of meditation. Practice this technique every day, at first for just 5–10 minutes then building up to 20 minutes.

Using crystals during meditation enhances your connection to self and helps you dive in deeper while you're meditating.

### What you need

One or more meditation crystals or gems (*see above*).

## What to do

◊ Find a quiet space and sit comfortably and still. Choose one or more crystals or gems to hold in your hands, wear or place around you. Now clear your thoughts. Relax your facial muscles and close your eyes (you'll be able to meditate with your eyes open when you're more experienced).

◊ Breathe in deeply through your nose, inhaling down into your abdomen, then slowly exhale through your mouth until your lungs are empty. Focus only on your breath until your mind is cleared, then focus on the energies of the crystals.

This method will help you to learn to quieten your mind. Practicing keeping your focus on energy is a great way to start building your awareness of the energies of the world around you, and will help in amplifying your Magickal skills.

## Candle meditation to clear the mind

Flames and candlelight can quickly hypnotize and create a state of trance, making it easy to be transported to another realm. Witches consult flames for answers, using them as a form of divination known as firegazing. However, for the following technique we're using a flame to clear our minds. This practice is best done in a dark or dimly lit room.

### What you need

A candle scented with frankincense, myrrh, cedar, lavender, palo santo, sage, or mugwort essential oil

### What to do

◊ Place the candle as close to eye level as possible; if you're sitting on the floor set the candle on the floor 3–4 feet in front of you.

◊ Sit comfortably and relax your body using the breathing technique I shared in the previous meditation. Bring your attention to the flame then soften your gaze and continue to meditate – for 10 minutes when you first practice this method, building up to 20–30 minutes as you become more skilled.

## Chant meditation to aid focus

A chant is a sound, a word, or a phrase that you repeat slowly in a rhythmic way while you meditate. Many find that the repetition helps to clear the mind and block out any noise around them.

### What to do

◊ Find a quiet space and sit comfortably. Choose your chant, sound, or phrase to repeat. It can be anything you like. Some I have heard include 'Omm, I am light,' 'I am powerful,' and 'Earth, air, fire, water,' and even humming, but the more personal it is and the more you feel connected to it, the better.

◊ Close your eyes, focus on your breathing then start your chanting. Go slowly and find a comfortable rhythm. Focus on nothing else but the sound and vibrations of your chant. Continue for 10–20 minutes.

## Potion to aid meditation

I created this special tea-infusion potion to help myself meditate. Drink it about 10 minutes before you meditate.

### What you need

I teaspoon dried blue lotus

I teaspoon fennel seeds

I teaspoon dried peppermint

I teaspoon dried rose petals

I teaspoon dried lavender

I tablespoon dried lemon balm

Milk, preferably nut-based, to taste

Honey, to taste

Alcohol, to taste (optional and only for those of legal age)

### What to do

◊ Put your dried ingredients in a teapot then add 1 cup (250ml) freshly boiled water. Add a little milk, honey, and, if desired, a little alcohol such as vodka or rum.

## Visualization

Visualization helps you to manifest your intentions by using your imagination. I'm sure you've daydreamed before and thought of yourself with a different look or in a different place, role-playing some fantastical story in your mind. If so, you already know how to tap in to this powerful technique.

Choose the form of meditation that works best for you, and once your mind is clear start your visualization. Imagine whatever it is you wish to manifest — for instance, if you want to manifest healing, visualize yourself already healed.

The most effective visualization involves all five senses: focus on what you can see, smell, taste, hear, and touch. Transport yourself to that place and actually live it. This technique can work for almost anything; it just takes time and practice.

# GROUNDING

To be grounded is to be energetically centered; to have channeled your energy so that you feel focused, balanced, and strong. Without being grounded you may experience unwanted feelings or behaviors: you may feel disconnected, physically or emotionally drained, irritable, worried, restless, or anxious for no real reason. This can cloud your intentions when manifesting. Grounding is essential to Magick and to your craft, and is extremely beneficial in life in general. It's a way to reinforce your connection to Mother Earth.

## Grounding practices

Try any of these practices at least once a day to experience a deeper connection to the Earth and to yourself.

## *Rooting*

Rooting is a simple grounding technique in which you visualize roots coming out of you and into the Earth. You can do it standing or sitting.

◊ Close your eyes and take three deep breaths. Now focus on the base of your spine. If you're sitting, visualize roots coming out of your spine and traveling down into the Earth; if you're standing, visualize the roots traveling down through your legs and out of the soles of your feet then into the ground.

◊ Journey with the roots deep into the ground, pushing and breaking through rock and dirt, deep into the core of our Earth.

◊ Once they're in the core, visualize your energy leaving your roots to feed our Mother until you feel calm, reconnected, and focused.

## *Earthing*

Connecting to the Earth's natural energy is a vital part of a Witch's life. Without this connection we cannot be connected to our Magick, our self, our truth – that we're all part of nature. Earthing also has many health benefits: research such as the studies carried out by the Earthing Institute has shown that getting close to nature can increase energy, improve sleep, reduce stress, and reduce the time to heal.

Spend time taking our Mother's medicine: walk barefoot on grass, sit under a tree, hug the tree, and don't forget to enjoy the feeling of sand, rock, and dirt – anything that requires you to have contact with our Mother.

## *Working with crystals and gems*

Crystals offer a fast and easy way to ground. Simply by holding a crystal in your hand you can remove any excess energy within yourself. Some of my favorite crystals for grounding are hematite, black obsidian, black tourmaline, and tiger's eye.

◊ Visualize your energy flowing through your hand and into the crystal.

◊ Focus on letting go of the energy that feels uncomfortable, negative, and overwhelming.

◊ Cleanse your crystals of the negative energies they have taken from you, either with a mugwort bundle or with incense – choose one from palo santo, cedar, or sandalwood. Alternatively, put the crystals in a bowl of salted water for at least an hour. You can also cleanse your crystals by placing them on the Earth.

### Listening to music

Music, particularly drumming, has a grounding effect. You can either listen to it or do some drumming yourself; either way, a steady rhythm is most effective. I love to listen to drumming while I'm doing my morning rituals. I also drum myself, on a small tambora, to elevate my spirit and ground myself to our Mother. Your drumming doesn't have to be elaborate; you can drum on anything you like or have available to you.

### Eating grounding foods

Foods that grow directly from the Earth – particularly vegetables – can help to ground you. Try to include grounding foods in your daily diet.

### Using essential oils, incense, and herbs

The scent of essential oils, incense, and herbs can all help you to ground. My favorites include vetiver, patchouli, angelica root, ylang ylang, rosewood, cinnamon, and frankincense, all of which can be found in at least one of the above forms. I also make a tea with the herbs and drink this to help me ground.

## Potion for grounding and centering

This potion is easy to make and works wonderfully to help release stress and anxiety, and to help you center. Put some in the bath or on your skin (always perform a skin-patch test first, to test for any adverse reaction) or use it to anoint candles.

### What you need

A 10ml vial

A base oil such as jojoba oil (enough to fill the vial by three-quarters)

9 drops frankincense essential oil

9 drops lavender essential oil

9 drops cedar essential oil

### What to do

◊ Add all of the oils to the vial, put the top on firmly and shake to combine the ingredients — that's it! Whenever you need to ground, release stress, or come back to self, put 1–2 drops of the oil on your wrists, back of the neck, or temples, or increase all the quantities proportionally so you can put 2–4fl oz (60–120ml) in the bath.

# RAISING ENERGY

In order to work Magick, you need to learn how to raise the energy required to manifest the intentions of your spells.

Ever since I was a little girl I've been able to raise energy using only my life force, but this can be very draining and isn't recommended for beginners. Instead, I recommend you raise energy with the help of tools such as crystals, chanting, and the Elements. It really isn't that hard – as usual, it just takes practice.

Raising energy requires two things: visualization and connection – connecting to the Earth and all that is, and being able to form energy using your mind. However, before you can raise energy effectively you need to meditate, to clear your mind, and enter a trance-like state.

The following methods for raising energy are mainly simple practices using the Earth's Elements. The last example is a more advanced method, should you need it.

Take your time, focus hard, be patient — and don't give up. Practice a little every day, whenever you can. Remember, there is already energy deep within your bones, because you're energy yourself.

With all methods of raising energy, be sure to thank the energies, Elements or spirits involved. You must also ground yourself (*see page 61*) to ensure a solid foundation on the Earth — a source of both energy and safety.

 ### Visualization for raising earth energy

Remember the grounding method where you grew roots into the Earth to release your energy (*see page 62*)? This exercise reverses that process so that you can borrow energy from our Mother.

### What to do

◊ Sit or stand on any patch of the Earth — grass, rock, dirt, or whatever you can find.

◊ Visualize roots coming out of the base of your spine and into the Earth. Journey with the roots deep into the ground and onward to the Earth's core.

◊ Visualize the core as a huge orb of energy pulsing and rotating. Sink your roots into that orb and draw up its energy through your roots and all the way inside you. I visualize this energy as blue in color, filling my entire body. Stop once you feel energized.

◊ If you feel lightheaded or overwhelmed, you took too much energy. Simply return some by using the grounding exercise.

◊ Now you can use the energy you've drawn up into your body to work your Magick. However, if you've been doing this exercise for practice alone, return all of the energy using the rooting exercise, thanking the Earth for sharing her energy with you.

##  Visualization for raising air energy

We can use the Element of air by building orbs of energy.

### What to do

◊ Go outside or next to an open window. Close your eyes, take a few deep breaths, and focus on calming your body and clearing your mind.

◊ Imagine the air going into your body as blue light, forming a pulsating blue orb in the center of your body, right behind your belly button, with blue lightning erupting inside it.

◊ Place your right hand over your belly button until you feel a magnetic pull from your palm to the orb. Visualize the orb moving out of your body and into your palm. Slowly extend your arm all the way out toward the right and release the orb. Imagine it rotating in that spot in the air. It will stay there until you use it.

◊ Repeat several times, placing the orbs around you in the same way. You can use the orbs of energy whenever you're doing any Magick. Simply grab them and place them into your work or imagine them floating down to you.

◊ If you're doing this for practice only, release the orbs either by taking them in your hand and blowing them back into the air, or laying them on the Earth and visualizing them sinking into the ground.

 ### Visualization for raising fire energy

You can draw energy from a candle, a backyard fire pit or any other form of fire. However, you have to be careful how much you take because fire is a wild, untamed energy that builds up quickly and can feel a bit overwhelming once you harness it.

The most accessible source of fire energy is sunlight; you can draw energy from the Sun just from being in its presence (but remember that you must never, ever look directly at the Sun, even through sunglasses).

Here is my favorite method for harnessing the Sun's energy.

## What to do

◊ Stand in direct sunlight (eyes away from the Sun) and visualize a clear crystal orb above your head. Raise your left hand to the sun and your right to the orb, with your palm turned toward it.

◊ Focus on your breath for a moment until you've cleared your mind. Now feel the energy of the Sun, pull it toward the palm facing it, and visualize the Sun's golden energy coming out through your other palm and into the orb.

◊ When you feel the orb beaming and pulsing with fire energy, bring your hands down and take a few deep breaths before using the orb in your work.

◊ To release this energy, simply use a grounding technique (*see page 61*).

## Visualization for raising water energy

Water energy is one of the most calming and loving energies and I often use it when I need embracing. You can draw energy from a glass of water, a bath, a waterfall, or the ocean – any type of water. The easiest and most convenient method of harnessing water energy uses a bowl of water, though you can use this technique with any other water too.

### What you need

A medium-size bowl filled with cold water

### What to do

◊ Sit down with the bowl of water directly in front of you. Close your eyes and take a few deep breaths to clear your mind.

◊ Place your hands in the water and relax them. Start to visualize the water vibrating around your hands and glowing with a beautiful white light. Allow your hands to take in the water's energy and, with it, the energy from the white light.

◊ Once you feel the energy pulsating in your hands, lift them out of the water and imagine them glowing brilliant white and emitting calming, loving energy. You can use this energy in your craft or for self-healing.

For instance, if you feel sad, place your hands over your heart and imagine the white light moving into it until your heart is glowing with the energy.

◊ If you want to release water energy without using it, use a grounding technique (*see page 61*).

 ## Ritual for raising a Cone of Power

This Magickal ritual for raising energy is most often carried out within a group or coven, but this example explains how to do it alone with the help of your ancestors and guides.

### What to do

◊ Cleanse yourself and your space. I would suggest lighting the candles or incense I recommend for grounding purposes (*see page 64*) so that you keep connection to the Earth during this practice. I like to light incense I'm familiar with so if at any point I need to bring myself back to self I can focus on the scent.

◊ You can either stand or sit for this process. Close your eyes and start to pray for or call upon your guides and ancestors to assist you. You can do this out loud or in your head. Take three very deep breaths and relax. Sit up straight and visualize a ball of energy in the center of your body, right behind your belly button. Allow this ball to pulsate and to grow a little every time you take a regular breath. Focus hard on this energy and contain it within the ball. (Most Witches I know like to visualize an electric-blue light for this energy.) Once you have control over the energy, imagine it growing outward and connecting with your guides and ancestors. Visualize their energy interlacing with yours.

◊ Now visualize a bright white cord of energy slithering from your core, up through your spine and out of the top of your head until it's about six feet the air. Visualize this happening to all of the guides and ancestors in the circle too, and all of the cords meeting at a center point, creating a point-up cone.

◊ Visualize this energy slowly starting to spin clockwise. Provided you feel in control, start to visualize the energy cone spinning faster and faster until it's creating a sort of inverted vortex.

◊ To use this energy, focus your intent and send the energy from the point of the cone into the Magick you're working.

# MANIFESTATION

**M**anifestation is simply the ability to attract what it is you're asking for. It's extremely important in Witchcraft: it's the conjuring of desires, the ability to make things happen. Since the beginning of time Witches have called on their energy, thoughts, and beliefs, along with laws of the universe, to manifest the outcome of their spells and Magickal workings.

## Candle spell for manifestation

To make this spell work you need to be able to cleanse the space, ground, raise energy, and focus on the intent. I have specified using a pull-out candle (one that sits inside a glass jar) so it can remain lit overnight with less risk of being knocked over. This spell is very dear to me and I hope it works wonders for you.

## What you need

A small handbell

A small bowl

1 teaspoon dried cornflower

1 teaspoon High John the Conqueror root powder

1 teaspoon dried goldenseal

1 teaspoon dried yellow dock

1fl oz (30ml) basil essential oil

1fl oz (30ml) patchouli essential oil

Paper and black pen

A white pull-out candle

A strand of your hair or a drop of your menstrual blood, or both – and if you're not menstruating use three nail clippings

Citrine and clear quartz crystals

## What to do

◊ First, clear and cleanse your space and yourself (*see page xvi*), then ring the bell three times to move the energy around the room.

◊ Set out your spell items and sit or stand in front of them. Now relax, close your eyes, and breathe deeply three times. Ground yourself and then raise the energy in the room.

◊ Make an anointing oil by mixing the herbs and essential oils in the bowl.

◊ With the pen, write on one side of the paper exactly what you want to manifest, right down to the tiniest detail.

◊ Now lightly spread a dash of the herb mixture over all of your words — no worries if it smears the ink; the point is to get the mixture to lightly touch all of your words.

◊ Fold the paper in half, folding the furthest edge toward you first. This will bring what you desire into your life. Set the paper aside.

◊ Take the candle out of its container, hold it in your hands, and enchant it by speaking your intention into it — you can say what you wrote or just ask it to bring you what you want. To call in what you desire, dip your finger into the herb mixture and smooth it all over the candle in a downward motion from top to bottom. Keep your desire in mind as you anoint the candle: visualize it, live it, and bring it into your presence so that those energies are soaked up by the candle.

◊ Next take the strand of your hair and wet it with your menstrual blood if you have some; this blood is extremely powerful and will help hold your essence. If you don't have any menstrual blood, use three nail clippings instead of the hair and wet them with your saliva.

◊ Wrap your hair around the candle or, if using nail clippings, push the clippings into the top of the candle, around the wick. Put the candle back in its container and take a moment to feel the energies around you. Take a deep breath in and blow slowly onto the unlit candle to seal it with your inner Magick.

◊ Set the candle by a window so that it can soak up the Moon's energies, and leave it until sunrise.

◊ Cleanse the surrounding space and yourself again — but don't cleanse the candle. Ground yourself and sit for a moment while you come back to self.

◊ At sunrise the next morning, bring the candle to your altar or anywhere else you like. Take three deep breaths and with the last breath blow slowly around the candle container to seal the Moon's energy into the candle. Place your note under the candle and arrange the crystals around it.

◊ The candle is now ready to light, and to manifest what you desire you should let it burn all the way down.

# Amplifying Your Inner Sense

When I was three or four years old, I realized that something inside me wanted to help and guide me. It began with feelings about other people, then about places, and there were things I knew instinctively, without knowing how or why. I now know this was my intuition — that inner sense, the higher intelligence to which we all have access. It became so strong that I started having visions and getting messages from every direction, both from within me and from outside. I believe that my intuition is as strong as it is now because as a child I believed it to be my best friend. It was the only thing that truly took care of me. I always paid attention and listened to it, and it got me where I am today.

Your intuition guides you through life, helping you to make the right choices and to avoid things or people that aren't good for you. Amplifying this inner sense is an important aspect of the Magickal craft. The craft can be unpredictable, so you need to have your wits about you and be able to feel what's happening, or about to happen. Experienced Witches also use their intuition, along with the enormous amount of knowledge and expertise they have accumulated, to create spells, remedies, and potions according to what feels right.

In today's modern world we tend to rely on outside sources more than our inner senses. But there are a few simple and fun practices you can do to reconnect with your intuition in your day-to-day life.

## Psychometry spell for developing psychic abilities

Psychometry is the art of learning about objects through touch. This exercise makes a great starting point for developing psychic abilities.

### What you need

A few small, random objects collected from friends who can later verify facts you feed back (good examples include old jewelry, old toys, keys, or anything else made from metal)

A tray

## What to do

◊ Place the objects on the tray within reach of where you're sitting. Get comfortable and take a few deep breaths to clear your mind.

◊ To raise energy, rub your hands together until you feel the warmth of the energy on your palms. Now take an object from the tray and hold it in your hands. Close your eyes, focus on your breathing for a moment, then direct your attention to the object.

◊ Focus on what you feel, see, hear, or smell, and let the object gradually connect with you. Consider simple questions to get your intuitive juices flowing: 'Does this object belong to a child or an adult?' 'Is the owner male or female?' 'Is the most recent owner of this object dead or alive?' Don't think about getting the answer wrong or right — the point is to pay attention to what your inner senses are trying to communicate to you. If you don't get anything, it's okay — this is why you're practicing. Be patient and be still.

◊ To help stay completely focused on the object rather than memorizing your thoughts, record yourself speaking about each object, or get someone to write your comments down for you.

◊ Go over your results with the friends who lent you the objects to see how accurate you were. If you missed the mark, don't worry! It takes time, but with repeated practice your intuition will amplify.

~~~

# Crystal grid spell for amplifying intuition

Crystal grids are specific patterns in which you arrange crystals to attract powerful intentions. The grids help to amplify the crystals' properties, including their power. The beauty of crystal grids is that you can use them for practically any intention. You can copy the grid opposite onto a surface of your choice, buy one ready-made, or download and print an image from the internet if this is permitted.

Using this spell requires the intuition you already have because it's up to you to choose where the crystals are placed. There's no right or wrong way to do this. Just take your time and really focus on the energies you're creating by using the grid.

*Sample crystal grid*

## What you need

6–12 small to medium crystals of up to three different kinds — choose from clear quartz, lapis lazuli, amethyst, aquamarine, or celestite

A crystal grid

## What to do

◊ Use your intuition to choose the crystal you feel has the greatest power and place this in the center of the grid. This is known as the master crystal. Continue to use your intuition to place the remaining crystals on the grid.

◊ To activate the grid, move your hand above the crystals. Imagine a beam of light connecting each crystal to the next, linking them all together. Focus on this light as it moves through all the crystals. Now hold your hand over the master crystal and feel all the energy centering there as a beacon for your intents and desires.

◊ Place your grid in a safe space, and if at any time you sense the grid needs to be charged up you can simply reactivate it by cleansing the crystals and repeating the activation process.

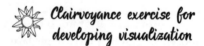

## Clairvoyance exercise for developing visualization

One of the most important keys to developing your inner sense for clairvoyance is visualization. This practice using playing cards is one I love to play with my children and friends, though you can also do it on your own.

### What you need

A pack of playing cards

Paper and pen

## What to do

◊ Choose five cards at random, lay them out, and study them for 10 seconds. Close your eyes and try to keep their images in your mind. Now have your friends remove the cards from view.

◊ Visualize the cards and write down what they were — the suit and the pattern or character. Ask your friends to reveal the cards to see if you're correct.

◊ With time the game will get easier, so keep challenging yourself: try recalling 10 cards in 10 seconds, and keep building from there.

# THE MOON AND
# THE WITCH

Timing in the Witch's craft is of great importance, and different phases of the Moon during each lunar cycle can significantly impact a spell or other Magickal workings. Some may say they don't have the time to wait for a particular phase, and that's fine; it's up to each Witch how they practice. But I have found that living by the Moon helps me to align with the natural flow of life, and the right Moon phase can offer a huge boost to my Magick.

A lunar cycle takes around 29½ days, during which the Moon passes through eight distinct phases. On the following pages I share with you the significance of each phase, and the intents and desires whose spells are most effective during those phases. I also suggest the best crystals to use. You can put these on your altar, arrange them around a candle (or press them into the top of one), or use them in spells that call for particular types of crystal.

Remember that Magick works differently for everyone. If you find that certain spells work best during a different phase, do them then instead — it's all part of building your own awareness and knowledge so that can create your own version of the craft.

*Phases of the Moon*

## ● New Moon

New Moons mark the beginning of the lunar cycle, making them perfect for Magick that sets new intentions that you wish to birth into reality. The Earth's soil is at its most fertile during the New Moon because the Moon draws up water from deep down in the Earth, so it's an ideal time to plant seeds — not only in your garden but also in your life. The New Moon invites us to work Magick that calls for new beginnings, rebirth, and a fresh start.

**Effective spells:** renewal, release, love, new direction, personal improvement, manifestation

**Crystal or gem to work with:** aquamarine is a great choice if you're healing or trying to let go of the past.

##  Waxing Crescent Moon

This phase occurs from 3½–7 days after New Moon. The Moon appears to be growing, and that's just what its energies assist with — growth. It brings to light things that need improvement, especially things you don't want to face. This is the perfect Moon phase for focusing on self, so working on your Magickal practice and any other self-development during this phase will help you reach your highest potential. The Waxing Crescent Moon also taps into answers you have hidden deep within, which means it's a good time to have a deeper look into your feelings about everything in your life, especially relationships.

**Effective spells:** courage, motivation, inspiration, attitude adjustment, patience, healing

**Crystal or gem to work with:** rose quartz is ideal for this phase because its gentle, calm energy promotes love, especially self-love. It also brings passion, which can help attract a romantic relationship or improve your current one.

##  First Quarter Moon

This phase occurs from 7–10½ days after New Moon. The First Quarter Moon is all about attracting and drawing things in. I particularly like to use this time to find missing objects, pets, and people. Looking for a new job? New love? More money? This is the time to work that Magick.

**Effective spells:** luck, wealth, success, love, protection

**Crystal or gem to work with:** I always recommend the pyrite for attracting and manifesting your desires, especially if you feel you're not worthy of them. Pyrite helps bring wisdom when calling for abundance, particularly of money, in your life.

##  Waxing Gibbous Moon

This phase occurs from 10½–15 days after New Moon. Like the First Quarter Moon, the Waxing Gibbous Moon is a time for attracting, but more often for inner strength and motivation to complete tasks and achieve goals. I like to use it when I need to follow an exercise plan or diet, or to stop procrastinating.

**Effective spells:** determination, confidence, strength, focus, clarity

**Crystal or gem to work with:** carnelian helps release any fears or anxieties that may be stopping you from pushing toward your goals, tasks, or projects.

 **Full Moon**

This phase occurs from 15–18½ days after New Moon. The Full Moon occurs when it's centered between the Earth and the Sun. It brings in the strongest energies of all the phases, so many Witches save their biggest Magick for this time, putting aside smaller spells that can be done during less powerful phases.

**Effective spells:** spirituality, health, success, luck, change, psychic development, decision-making

**Crystal or gem to work with:** clear quartz matches the Full Moon perfectly: it's something of a chameleon and will support any purpose. Clear quartz is powerful, too, and can be used to amplify, release, attract, banish, and heal.

 **Waning Gibbous Moon**

This phase occurs from 3½–7 days after Full Moon. The Waning Gibbous Moon follows the Full Moon and is a great time to work on release and self-reflection. During this phase, take a good look at your life: is this where you

want to be right now? Where do you go from here, and how? Really focus on self-reflection and releasing what no longer serves you: troubles, blocks, distractions, and negative relationships with friends and partners.

**Effective spells:** release, opportunities, ending procrastination, bad habits, fears, negative emotions

**Crystal or gem to work with:** amethyst will help you to break bad habits and give you the will to stick to your intention.

##  Third Quarter Moon

This phase occurs from 7–10½ days after Full Moon. This phase of the Moon offers an opportunity to get to the root cause of a problem and to get rid of the blocks stopping you from moving forward. I find that divination works well during this phase and I use it to discover what changes I must make to remove these obstacles.

**Effective spells:** transitions, awareness, removing obstacles

**Crystal or gem to work with:** Magick during this phase requires bravery, and bloodstone's link to courage makes it ideal to work with in the Third Quarter phase; it's effective for pushing away obstacles and opening doors. It also increases power and strength, which will help you accomplish what you want.

**Waning Crescent Moon**

This phase occurs from 10½ days after Full Moon and continues to the beginning of the New Moon. As the Moon disappears from the night sky it's the time to work on some major banishing Magick — banishing negativity (including chaos), ghosts, stalkers, problems, stress, and illness. Witches also use this energy to rid the whole world of hidden evils.

**Effective spells:** banishment, binding (restricting others' actions), protection

**Crystal or gem to work with:** black tourmaline is an ideal choice for banishing. It repels lower frequencies of energy that may be harmful. It's also believed to protect against electromagnetic radiation, so it's no surprise that it repels other potential sources of harm as well.

# THE SEASONS
OF THE WITCH

Just as they follow the phases of the Moon, many Witches honor what I call the Seasons of the Witch — an annual cycle of four equinoxes based on astronomical events and four solstices (traditional pagan festivals), some of which are now Earth-bound festivals too. There are roughly two Seasons of the Witch for every Earth-bound season. Harnessing the energies from these Seasons while they're with us not only strengthens our connection to Mother Earth, but also amplifies our Magickal power.

Some Witches celebrate all eight Seasons, while others celebrate only the equinoxes or the solstices, or a selection of each. It's up to the individual what they celebrate, and as you develop your craft you too can decide which Seasons are right for you.

In this chapter you'll find essential information for every Season of the Witch and some of their key correspondences – objects such as herbs and crystals, plus colors and Magickal workings, that help you to harness a Season's energy to strengthen your Magickal power. For instance, dressing your altar with fabrics in the Season's colors, or burning corresponding herbs or incense, will help bring in the Season's energy. At your altar in particular, the correspondences will help to keep the energy flowing and clear stagnant energies – another way to amplify your Magick.

You don't have to use all of the correspondences, and not every Witch will use the same ones. Just choose the ones you think will best harness the season's energy for your own Magickal workings.

As well as giving you correspondences to choose from, I also suggest ways to celebrate each Season. You can make as much of these as you like, but even by adjusting your altar you're honoring and celebrating the Season, so just this simple act can be enough. It's up to you how you wish to honor the Seasons of the Witch.

## 🍁 Samhain

**Also known as:** All Hallows' Eve, Halloween

**When:** northern hemisphere 31 October; southern hemisphere 1 May

**Celebrates:** ancestors, spirits, those who have passed

**Energies:** death, rebirth, wisdom, essence of the night, communication, release, return

**Ideal spell for this time:** star anise psychic-amplifier and protection incense (*see page 200*)

Samhain is the best known of the Seasons of the Witch as it falls on Halloween, when even muggles come out and play on the Magickal side. The main purpose of Samhain is to celebrate the natural cycle of death and rebirth. Its name comes from the Gaelic word for 'summer's end,' and it marks the point at which we enter the darker part of the solar year. At Samhain we celebrate and honor the dead, our ancestors, and spirits. With the veil between their realm and ours at its thinnest, this is the time we can most easily communicate with them.

## Correspondences

### MAGICKAL WORKINGS

Communion with the dead, protection, candle Magick, past life, ancestors, psychic powers, release of bad habits, banishing, self, uncrossing (removing hexes)

### ALTAR CHANGES

**Symbols:** pumpkins, jack o' lanterns, apples, corn, gourds, fall flowers, dried leaves, crows, ghosts, cobwebs, broomsticks, cauldrons, bones, lanterns, candles, the Moon

**Colors:** black, orange, red, white, gold

**Herbs and other plants:** mugwort, garlic, rosemary, catnip, nettle, bay leaf, marigold, rue

**Incense:** frankincense, myrrh, copal, sandalwood, amber, wormwood, mugwort, patchouli

**Crystals and gems:** black obsidian, bloodstone, jet, hematite, onyx, smoky quartz, carnelian

## WAYS TO CELEBRATE

**Honor the dead:** Honor the departed by setting up a special altar on which you place food, drink, pictures, and other items that may have belonged to the departed, or that hold meaning associated with them. Some Witches honor the dead by leaving offerings, such as food, outside their door for any spirits who may come by. Lighting candles and leaving them outside your door or window will invite departed loved ones into the home.

**Silent Supper:** The Silent Supper, or Dumb Supper, is a popular tradition around the world to celebrate Samhain. The meal honors the dead by being taken in silence, with the diners taking care to eat and drink quietly as well as refraining from speaking. It's even important to clear the dishes without making any noise. I've known many Silent Suppers to include a table setting, complete with food, for all those who have departed. Remember that this is a sacred dinner, so light candles and set a peaceful atmosphere for the event.

##  Yule

**Also known as:** Yuletide, winter solstice

**When:** northern hemisphere December 20–23; southern hemisphere June 20–23

**Celebrates:** the coming of the Sun

**Energies:** reflection, rebirth, transformation, creativity

**Ideal spell for this time:** catnip healing spell (*see page 184*)

Winter solstice is the longest night of the year and is celebrated around the world for the coming of the Sun, when the darkness of midwinter begins to transform into the light of spring and summer. It's a time of deep spiritual reflection for the light that is to come.

### *Correspondences*

Magickal workings

Self-development, self-love, healing, reflection, binding (restricting others' actions)

## Altar changes

**Symbols:** yule log, decorated tree, mistletoe, poinsettia, pine cones, candles, evergreens, holly, wreaths, bells, lights, angels, ivy

**Colors:** gold, silver, red, green

**Herbs and other plants:** milk thistle, evergreens, holy basil, holly, rosemary, mistletoe, oak, cedar, poinsettia, ivy, juniper, cinnamon, amaryllis, lemon balm

**Incense:** pine, cedar, juniper, rosemary, bayberry, cinnamon, frankincense, birch

**Crystals and gems:** ruby, diamond, emerald, garnet, quartz, selenite

## Ways to celebrate

**Solstice walk:** I love being in nature at this time of year, especially with my children. We go to woods or mountains, and walk with lanterns in our hands, gathering nature's little treasures for our altars and Yule decorations. We hug the older trees, feed any little animals that may be hungry, and sit and drink cocoa or tea in the presence of our Mother, Earth.

**Casting candles:** Casting candles is a group ritual my ancestors passed down to me. Gather your circle and set a large bowl in the center of the group. Each person writes on a bay leaf the most important thing they wish to manifest in the year ahead. They then light a candle, place the bay leaf in the bowl, and sprinkle a dash of cinnamon over it. All candles are then set in a circle around the bowl and left to burn all the way down. The notes are then taken and buried in dirt.

##  Imbolc

**Also known as:** Candlemas

**When:** northern hemisphere 1–2 February; southern hemisphere 31 July–1 August

**Celebrates:** purification, the coming of spring

**Energies:** conception, renewal, dedication, planning, setting intentions, goals

**Ideal spell for this time:** wood betony new-beginnings foot oil (*see page 196*)

The festival of Imbolc celebrates purification, the approach of spring, and the awakening of the goddess in the Earth. It's a time to prepare for the planting season and a time to declutter and organize, and to clean and bless our sacred spaces, altars, and tools.

## *Correspondences*

### MAGICKAL WORKINGS

Growth, cleansing, purification, manifesting

### ALTAR CHANGES

**Symbols**: white flowers, white candles, Brigid's cross, potted bulbs

**Colors**: white, red, green, brown

**Herbs and other plants**: angelica, basil, bay, laurel, clover, tansy, willow, dandelion, chamomile, celandine, heather, all white flowers

**Incense**: basil, rosemary, myrrh, frankincense, vanilla

**Crystals and gems**: amethyst, garnet, onyx, moonstone, turquoise

### WAYS TO CELEBRATE

**Spring cleaning**: Imbolc is a time for purification, so we clean our homes, open windows, and tend to our plants. We also hang chimes and set out white flowers. Many Imbolc rituals honor the goddess Brigid with candlelight and woven ornaments. Since Imbolc doesn't involve feasting, use the time to enjoy the light coming into the home and into the soul.

**Setting goals:** A wise Witch knows to plan ahead, so grab a journal and start to make a list of things you want to do or accomplish in the coming year. Start with the most important and plan how you'll tackle each goal as it comes up.

 **Ostara**

**Also known as:** spring equinox

**When:** northern hemisphere March 19–22; southern hemisphere September 20–23

**Celebrates:** the beginning of spring, new life, rebirth, love, fertility

**Energies:** birth, love, sexuality, fertility, beginnings, power, strength, completion

**Ideal spell for this time:** wheat manifesting mail spell (*see page 204*)

Many celebrate this well-known festival, which most know as Easter. Ostara honors the beginning of spring, new life, and rebirth, love, and fertility. At Ostara we take notice of the things that may have shifted out of balance and revisit our priorities.

## *Correspondences*

### MAGICKAL WORKINGS

Abundance, manifesting, balance, getting rid of what no longer serves you

### ALTAR CHANGES

**Symbols:** spring flowers, the Green Man, fairies, butterflies

**Colors:** pastels, yellow, orange, lavender, green

**Herbs and other plants:** angelica, basil, bay leaf, clover, tansy, willow, dandelion, snowdrop, crocus, trillium, heather, iris, rose

**Incense:** jasmine, rosemary, rose, lavender, ylang ylang, copal

**Crystals and gems:** amethyst, rose quartz, aquamarine, moonstone, turquoise

### WAYS TO CELEBRATE

**Plant seeds – with intentions:** As you put a seed into the earth, whisper an intention you wish to manifest.

**Chocolate eggs – with intentions:** This concept is similar to the New Year's Eve tradition of eating 12 grapes and setting an intention into each one before you eat it. For this version, gather 12 small chocolate eggs, and for each egg, take a moment to reflect then set an intention into it and eat it. That's it!

##  Beltane

**Also known as:** May Day

**When:** northern hemisphere 30 April–1 May; southern hemisphere 31 October

**Celebrates:** sexuality, sacrifice, rebirth, union of the god and goddess

**Energies:** masculine, feminine

**Ideal spell for this time:** cinnamon love-attracting sachet (*see page 153*)

Beltane is a passionate, sexual day that celebrates the union of the god and goddess. Many orgies are held on this day but you're unlikely to run into one at a ritual because they tend to be discreetly kept within trusted groups. Beltane is a popular time for lovers to propose and for the renewing of vows.

### Correspondences

#### MAGICKAL WORKINGS

All Magick will be powerful today since the energies are high and hold the essences of both the feminine and masculine.

## Altar changes

**Symbols**: flowers, flower crowns, wreaths, red or pink candles

**Colors**: green, blue, pink, purple, red

**Herbs and other plants**: wormwood, broom, elderflower, foxglove, hawthorn, catnip, marigold, mugwort, primrose, thyme, horny goat weed, ashwagandha

**Incense**: rose, juniper, clove, bergamot, violet, vanilla

**Crystals and gems**: rose quartz, red aventurine, sapphire, peridot, amber

## Ways to celebrate

**Bonfires**: Beltane is a time to let go and just be, so light a bonfire and wildly jump and dance around it. Laugh loudly and heartily. Dancing round a maypole is lots of fun, if you can get access to a maypole and find enough friends and a leader to join you.

**Home comforts**: Rather have a quiet night at home with your love? Then celebrate Beltane by cooking together, crafting, or putting flowers in each other's hair — be lighthearted, have fun, and be flirty and playful.

**Litha**

**Also known as:** summer solstice

**When:** northern hemisphere 20–23 June; southern hemisphere 20–23 December

**Celebrates:** virility, growth, success

**Energies:** growth, healing, love

**Ideal spell for this time:** ginger root project-completion bath spell (*see page 168*)

Litha is the longest day of the year. It's the day when the Sun God is at the peak of his virility and the Sun Goddess is with child. It's the time of year when crops are growing heartily and the Earth is fertile and happy.

## *Correspondences*

### Magickal workings

Communication with nature spirits, love, protection, healing, wealth

### Altar changes

**Symbols:** the Sun, yellow candles, flowers (particularly roses and sunflowers), river stones, seashells, sand, water recently taken from a river or the ocean

**Colors**: green, yellow, gold, red

**Herbs and other plants**: nettle, vervain, lavender, thyme, fern, yarrow, St John's wort, oak, fennel

**Incense**: sandalwood, frankincense, myrrh, palo santo, amber, copal, mountain sage, musk

**Crystals and gems**: emerald, jade, gold, sunstone

## Ways to celebrate

**Gathering**: Head out into nature and enjoy a gathering with friends, perhaps a drum circle. Have a picnic and revel in the beauty of our Mother, Earth, while the Sun blesses us with its enchanting rays.

**Sun water**: On the evening before Litha, pour some water into a bowl or jar and arrange around it some summer flowers and a few crystals or gems (*see above*). Leave the bowl or jar outside or by a window until the Sun sets. The water will now hold the energies of this day and can be used in your teas, spells, baths, and so on.

## 🍁 Lammas

**Also known as**: Lughnasadh

**When**: northern hemisphere 1 August; southern hemisphere 2 February

**Celebrates:** first harvest, abundance

**Energies:** abundance, wealth, success, gratitude

**Ideal spell for this time:** alfalfa buried-apple spell (*see page 177*)

At Lammas we honor and celebrate the first harvest of the year, the reaping of wheat, barley, rye, oats, and hops. We gather and give thanks for the abundance of these staple foods to see us through the coming year.

## *Correspondences*

### Magickal workings

Abundance, prosperity, success, wealth, money, good fortune, transformation

### Altar changes

**Symbols:** baskets of bread; cauldrons of yellow, red or orange flowers; corn; fresh herbs; hanging bunches of dried herbs; ears of wheat, barley or rye

**Colors:** orange, yellow, green, brown, bronze

**Herbs and other plants:** wheat, barley, oats, rye, hops, corn stalks, sunflowers, calendula, mint, oak, hollyhock, meadowsweet

**Incense**: eucalyptus, rose, rosehip, rosemary, lemon balm, safflower

**Crystals and gems**: emerald, carnelian, citrine, cat's eye

<u>WAYS TO CELEBRATE</u>

**Craft a corn doll**: Honor the Grain Goddess by making a corn doll to represent the harvest. As you make her, weave in intentions of gratitude. Many people dress and name their doll then keep her until the spring, when they plant her with the new corn, returning her to the Earth.

**Bake bread**: I find baking bread both therapeutic and Magickal, and it really isn't as hard as you'd think. Using grain is an ideal way to honor Lammas, as is the addition of fresh herbs — I love to add rosemary and thyme.

## 🍁 Mabon

**Also known as**: autumn equinox

**When**: northern hemisphere 20–23 September; southern hemisphere 20–23 March

**Celebrates**: second harvest, aging, death, the spirit world

**Energies**: reflection, contemplation

**Ideal spell for this time:** lemongrass intuition-amplifier wash (*see page 202*)

As the days begin to shorten and we prepare for the coming of winter, we celebrate Mabon to honor the second harvest of the year and the changing seasons. We also honor the cycles of aging and death, and of the spirit world, along with the Green Man, the God of the Forest, and the aging goddess as she passes from mother to crone.

## *Correspondences*

### Magickal workings

Prosperity, protection, balance, acceptance, remembrance, divination

### Altar changes

**Symbols:** pine cones, acorns, corn, apples, animal horns, ivy, red poppies, garlands, ears of wheat, wreaths, rattles, all autumn flowers

**Colors:** red, maroon, orange, brown, gold

**Herbs and other plants:** honeysuckle, marigold, milkweed, cedar, pine, oak, acorns, benzoin, ferns, myrrh, tobacco, thistle

**Incense:** benzoin, cinnamon, myrrh, sweetgrass, oakmoss, patchouli

**Crystals and gems**: yellow agate, lapis lazuli, carnelian, sapphire

<u>WAYS TO CELEBRATE</u>

**Get prepared**: Plan ahead and gather herbs and flowers to dry for your spells, tinctures, and Magickal workings in the colder months ahead. Now's the time to stock up, Witches.

**Enjoy autumn**: Witches always feel a pull from within to indulge in all that autumn brings – to gather leaves, pick pumpkins, and eat and drink everything warm and comforting to our souls. Remember to offer libations to the trees, adorn the burial sites of those who have passed, and thank the flowers and the older trees for their medicine and wisdom.

How you celebrate the Seasons of the Witch, and how you use their correspondences, is up to you. Get creative and have fun. Most importantly, start to connect to the Elements and to our Mother, Earth. You're not living *with* nature, you *are* nature.

PART THREE

# PRACTICAL MAGICK

# CONNECTING WITH
# YOUR INNER WITCH

One of the things from my childhood that I'm most grateful for is the journal that my mother handed to me when I was seven years old. It was blue and had Disney's Little Mermaid on the cover. (I didn't like the cover, but I didn't say so.) I quickly ran into my room and shut myself in my secret hiding spot in the closet. I lit a lantern I kept there, opened the journal, and just stared at it. The only thing I could think to put in it was a drawing. So I drew some stars and a giant Moon. I drew the graveyard across the street from where I lived and added some ghosts. I took a hard look at what I'd drawn and for some strange reason I felt compelled to write the words 'Full Moon' next to the Moon, and then I labeled everything I had drawn: 'Stars' next to the stars, 'Clouds,' next to the clouds, and so on.

It was completely new to me to label what I had drawn, and then I remembered the big old book my mother wrote in but never allowed me to touch. I ran to the kitchen to try to take a peek. When she wasn't looking, I took my chance… Wow! To my surprise, it was full of drawings with labels and writings. Without looking back at me (I swear she had eyes in the back of her head) she said, 'You can look, but don't touch. Don't copy, but create your own.' I asked her why she liked to draw vegetables and plants, and she said, 'I like to keep a record of the things that speak to me and the conversations we have.' I looked at her and thought, *You speak to celery? What could celery possibly have to say?*

From that moment I wrote all of my secrets and thoughts in my journal and drew the things I had conversations with — the bees, butterflies, trees, and spirits. I stuck into it random things I'd found and liked, especially those that spoke to me. I began to understand what that great big book was for, and from then on I kept what I now call a Witch's Journal.

# A BOOK OF
# SHADOWS AND
# A GRIMOIRE

Many Witches keep a Grimoire and a Book of Shadows. A Grimoire is a Witch's personal reference book of their own spells, potions, the tools they use in their craft, and the Magickal properties of crystals, candles, herbs, and plants that work best for them. It's a record of a Witch's own research and discoveries, and one they come back to whenever they need to revisit the information they have collected.

A Book of Shadows, meanwhile, is more like a Witch's diary, in which a Witch will record the experience and results of various Magickal practices, as well as dreams and their meanings, and other Magickal events.

Both books help to manifest and amplify a Witch's inner power and energy.

Don't let anyone tell you how to create your Book of Shadows or Grimoire; there is no wrong or right way. Just do what works best for you. You don't even need both, but if you do, you don't have to keep them separate. You can keep a Book of Shadows and add your research to it. This merger is what I like to call a Witch's Journal, and it's what I keep and carry wherever I go. I use a large, sturdy notebook and start another volume whenever I need to, although some Witches prefer to use a ring binder so they can add or remove pages as they wish.

Remember, no matter how you keep your records, either in a Book of Shadows, a Grimoire, or a Witch's Journal, they're sacred books and should be treated with love, care, and respect. No one should read or touch your book unless you give them permission. Keep it hidden and protected.

### Ritual for blessing your Book of Shadows, Grimoire, or Witch's Journal

Before you start your Book of Shadows, Grimoire or Witch's Journal, make sure you bless it, which will also bring it protection. You can do this even if you already have your book but haven't blessed it yet.

## What you need

Dried herbs — choose from basil or rue; or incense — choose from copal or frankincense

Your Book of Shadows, Grimoire, or Witch's Journal

A piece of cloth bigger than your book

A white candle

A small bowl of salt

## What to do

◊ Start by creating a sacred space free from negative energies. Sit somewhere quiet and keep some herbs, resin, or incense burning to encourage calming energies — or whichever energies you wish.

◊ Place the book in front of you on top of the cloth, cover side up, and with the shorter end nearest to you. Light the candle and place it to the right of the book. Place the bowl of salt on the left-hand side of the book.

◊ Now focus on yourself. Calm your body and clear your mind using any of the meditation practices in Part Two of this book. When you're ready, open your eyes and take a small handful of salt. Sprinkle the salt onto your book while saying out loud, or in your head, 'Book of my sacred, you are now cleansed. May your pureness keep, and your light hold.' Or say something of your own along these lines. Now turn the book over and repeat the process.

◊ Next, hold your right palm above the candle — not so close that you burn yourself but enough to feel its warmth. Close your eyes and hold your hand there for about 10 seconds. Now pick up the book with your left hand and place your right palm over the cover. Start to imagine the warmth and energy from your palm sinking into the book and filling it with light.

◊ When you're ready, say, 'In this book lives spirit and Magick. No one shall enter its sacred pages unless chosen. May it be protected by the power of the spells whispered upon it; the spells spilled from my own tongue and crafted from the heart. No harm shall come to this enchanted book of mine, for I have bestowed it with my Magick and sealed it by hand.' Again, these specific words are only an example.

## What to write in your Book of Shadows or Grimoire

It's entirely up to you when it comes to the contents of your Book of Shadows or Grimoire, but there are a few subjects that are included by most Witches.

Here are my top five must-haves.

## Correspondences

Correspondences are among the most important things to put in your book. These might be herbs and their uses, crystals and gems, colors, or the phases of the Moon (*see pages 88–93*).

## Magickal recipes and tools

I love to write down all of the Magickal recipes I create. When I started my book, I wrote down recipes I found in other books, but I now put in my own. Enter recipes for potions, spells, essential oils, remedies, your Magical workings, and so on, but only record those you've practiced yourself and that work for you. That said, I like to write Magickal recipes in my book then cross them out if they *don't* work, recording my experience. I then adjust them until they work just right. You can also include cookery recipes with Magickal properties, especially those celebrating special Magickal festivals. Also keep a record of your research on the tools you use for your craft.

## The Seasons and the Moon

It's extremely useful to be able to look up the phases of the Moon, their meanings, energies, and what Magick to work on during each phase. It's also a great idea to include notes about each of the Seasons of the Witch, and about important astrological events. Note down the spells, rituals, crafts, and so on for each Season.

### Personal findings

I'm not talking about Magickal research but about the very personal things you find, love, and cherish, such as flowers, feathers, pictures, or quotes – anything that really speaks to you. Glue, tape, or staple these items into your book and try to add the reason you chose them. The more personal this is, the better the energies will be.

### Signs and messages

I'm extremely aware of the messages and signs around me, and I keep a record of all of them. If I happen to think of something for which I need an answer or reassurance, and then a feather floats down in front of me and touches my nose, I would take that as a sign. I would then meditate on it and find the meaning through my guides and ancestors, then write it down in my book. Make it a habit to record your communication with spirits and ancestors. Keeping a record of what certain events turn out to mean to you is really important because signs and messages don't mean the same thing to everyone. Writing them down also helps you to remember them when your book isn't to hand.

# CREATING AN ALTAR

Every Witch needs a sacred space, usually an altar, where they can worship deities, ancestors, or whatever they like, and practice Magick. It's also a place to reflect, express gratitude, reset, center, and come back to self; a place that represents your purpose so that whenever you walk past it you're reminded to devote yourself to your craft and to self.

## A space that's yours

An altar should be as unique as the person creating it. It doesn't have to be fancy or house expensive tools; it can be as simple as just a candle and small trinkets that have meaning for you. Just focus on what's most important to you.

To create your altar, start by focusing on its location. It can be quite literally anywhere (though this may depend on the space you have available) as long as you know that neither you nor your altar will be disturbed. If you live with other people, you may choose to set up a barrier such as a curtain. When my four siblings and I were little, my mother kept her altar locked away from us in a closet. At college I kept my altar in a trunk under my bed and took it out when I wanted to. I kept it organized and wrapped my items carefully before putting them away again. (This is also a great method if you want to keep your craft to yourself.) You might find somewhere you can put up a shelf or set a small table. The top of a dresser or a space in a cabinet can work well too.

Just recently I met a mother and daughter who had converted their attic into their sacred space. How amazing is that? My nine-year-old son keeps his altar on his dresser in front of his fish tank, and I have a friend who keeps hers outside by a tree, surrounded by her garden. Just find what works best for you — and bear in mind that a sacred space doesn't need a permanent location; it can be changed as often as you like.

### What to put on your altar

Here are some ideas of items to keep on your altar or in your sacred space, though of course you can choose what means the most to you.

**Pictures and images:** As in many cultures and traditions, you may like to add photos, paintings, or figurines of gods, goddesses, saints, mentors, or ancestors who you're connected with or who mean something to you.

**Items with personal meaning:** It's important that you add things that are meaningful to you. It might be a piece of jewelry handed down to you, an item that belonged to one of your ancestors, a feather that came to you when you needed guidance, or crystals, gems, or seashells. You can include symbols of your religion too.

**Candles, smoke, and scents:** Lit candles, incense, essential oils, and burning herbs are often present on altars. Personally, I love all the Elements to be present on my altar, and I add or remove items to adjust the energy according to what I'm doing there on certain days. I also like to use scents that pertain to the time of year (*see pages 95–112*).

**Seasonal decoration:** I like altars to be decorated according to each season. This helps to harness the season's energy and amplifies the effect of your Magickal workings. For instance, for Yule add reds and greens to your altar, perhaps in your choice of candle color or the bowl in which you burn your herbs. Collect pine cones, make water from snow, and include these.

**Inspiration for focus:** Among my favorite things to include in my sacred space are plants, flowers, my journal, poetry, and other things that inspire me to stay focused. I have hung my favorite paintings and pictures there, too — anything that brings me back to who I am and reminds me of the spirit living within.

Spend at least 10 minutes at your altar or in your sacred space each day, praying or meditating, or just giving it some sort of attention. Always keep this space clean and organized, and cleanse it from negative energies as often as possible. Later in the book (*see page 202*) I've included a recipe for lemongrass intuition-amplifier wash which works really well for this.

# HARNESSING
# ANCESTRAL
# WISDOM

Ancestors provide great guidance, wisdom, and lessons, as well as great protection, healing, and growth. Connecting with your ancestors brings a deeper understanding of self and greater spirituality. It's important to connect to your ancestors for these reasons alone.

The type of ancestor you may be most familiar with is one who once had a physical form and a human experience. However, there are also Land Ancestors, who watch over a land to which they're connected. These are particularly important to those who still live on ancestral lands. There are also Spiritual Ancestors — ancestors who your soul has worked with for many lifetimes or who are connected to your lineage. These ancestors can be angels, gods, goddesses, guides, guardians from other planets, and so on. My favorite ancestors are our mountains, trees, plants, animals, rivers, and oceans, and our Mother Earth herself. I work with her every single day.

We all descend from Healers, wisewomen and wise men, medicine people (known today as herbalists), visionaries, activists, and warriors — we come from a mix of all our ancestors' prehistory lived as one with the Earth. They survived by being in tune with the natural environment, animals, the stars, the Moon, the land, and the spirits. Ancient knowing dwells within your being. It is and always will be a part of you, a spiritual enchantment walking alongside you.

The best way to harness ancestral wisdom is to commune directly with your ancestors. It's okay to feel nervous when beginning this journey. Remember that it takes practice, just like everything else, so don't give up; however, you may find that your ancestors are so eager to communicate with you that they start to connect right away. You may feel silly and have doubts, but if you reject those feelings and keep an open mind, invite calm energy, and allow yourself to feel without judgment, you'll notice the messages coming through. Give it a try: practice daily or as often as you can. If you're not comfortable doing this on your own, seek guidance from someone who has experience in this area.

## A shrine to your ancestors

Having an altar, or shrine, dedicated to your ancestors is a great way to honor and work with them, and to remember your connections with them. The ancestor altar operates between worlds and will house a lot of energy, so set it up where it won't disturb anyone — not in the bedroom, for example — and won't get disturbed by anyone else, particularly children or pets.

Your ancestor altar can look however you want it to. Follow your intuition and add things that have meaning. Here are a few ideas:

**Pictures** of your ancestors.

**Inherited objects** or other items that give you a connection to your ancestors.

**Sacred items** your ancestors would recognize. Some of my ancestors were Catholic Witches, so on my altar I have an antique Bible, a rosary, and images of saints they believed in. Other Witches in my family practiced Santeria, Hoodoo, and Shamanism. Meanwhile, I'm Cuban with African, Iberian, and Native American roots so my ancestor altar is spiritually very colorful and honors my forebears in many different ways.

**Light** from candles, lanterns, or sunshine. These make a great way to illuminate your altar, and though you can use them there every day if you wish, they make a particularly special way to celebrate the birthdays of your human ancestors, as well as seasonal festivals.

**Items connected to you**, either because they run through your roots or because your ancestors are pulling those items in. These might include crystals or gems, certain herbs, incense, plants, Elements, or art.

If you don't know who your ancestors are, just go with what feels right to you. The altar will be no less sacred. Trust me: your ancestors will let you know what they want.

## Protecting yourself

Before you practice any Magickal workings or even prepare to do so, you must protect yourself against any spirits who may not have your highest good in mind. It's unfortunate, but not all spirits are 'good' and you should not leave yourself open to them. You need to ensure that the connections you make are with those who have your back and have your best interest in mind.

Here are the simplest ways to keep yourself safe:

◊ **Cleanse the space** with the smoke of herbs or incense before and after your Magickal work to clear away any negative energy, or the energy of friends and family who have been in the vicinity (*see also page 139*).

◊ **Use crystals or charms** that have protective properties, such as obsidian, amethyst, or smoky quartz (*see also page 142*).

◊ **Light protective candles** — black or white ones give protection. Make sure you spiritually cleanse the candle before use (or buy candles that have been prepared for you), then hold the candle and recite a prayer or spell asking the candle protect you.

◊ **Be clear** about who is allowed in. Make it known that you only want to connect and communicate with spirits who are there to help and support you.

◊ **Set energy boundaries** by visualizing a sphere of light around you. Then announce, either out loud or in your head, what you'll allow into your sacred sphere. For instance, 'Only good shall enter this sphere. I do not allow negativity or anything that doesn't have my best interest in mind. I do not allow in any ill spirits, or anything or anyone with bad intentions.'

## Communicating with your ancestors

Communicating with your ancestors can be done in many ways, and as you explore this process you'll find out what works best for you.

The simplest way is to just ask: talk to your ancestors, and remember that they're always there and want to connect with you; they want to have a relationship with you, so just talking to them can be extremely effective. If you know the names of your ancestors, simply call on whoever it is you want to communicate with.

Some of us have more heightened senses and can quickly feel, hear, or even see our ancestors, but most of us need to refine these senses. The best way to do that is by paying attention to all the signs and not dismissing them. Listen to your intuition and stay aware.

This can take years of practice, so keep it basic at first and work your way up to more intense ritual practices. Do your research: consult with someone who has extensive experience of communicating with ancestors, and read some of the many books and articles available on this topic. The most important thing to remember is that this is a journey. Be patient, stay open-minded, take your time, and do as much or as little as you like. Remember also to practice protection, and don't mess with spirits you have no business in communicating with.

## *Making the first connection*

Making that first contact with your ancestors takes practice but it can be done using even the simple methods that follow, as long as you focus on both what's within you and outside you. It will eventually become clear where and how your ancestors are trying to communicate with you.

**Tune in:** To communicate with your ancestors, you need to learn how to tune in to them. This can come through sound, sight, feelings, or signs. Stay aware and record everything, especially dreams, visions, and any peculiar things that happen during your day.

**Meditate:** We discussed some techniques for meditation earlier in the book (*see pages 54–60*), so start meditating, Witches! The only difference here is that when you meditate for communicating, you need to make this clear to your ancestors before you start. You may want to repeat a phrase or a spell that enables this, or you might hold or surround yourself with crystals, incense, or candles that help you to tune in.

**Listen:** Ancestors and guides always show up; it's up to you to pay attention to the way they do it. Not all spirits are alike and not all of them communicate in the same way. Some are direct and some are like poets, so you need to read between the lines and *feel* their message rather than hear or see it. Your ancestors may come to you at times of great need or they may come in everyday moments. Pay attention to how you feel: sometimes you can sense that someone is there with you, a presence that isn't yours. Be alert to things that grab your attention, such as animals, numerical synchronicity, a sudden shift in the wind, or a rush of Magickal energy within you. The more you pay attention to these things, the stronger your senses will become and so, too, your communication with your ancestors and guides.

I've experienced my ancestors' wisdom in many forms and in all sorts of places. For instance, one night I stayed up late to write this book as it was the only time I could find. I was also in the process of opening my own shop, I had interviews and events to attend, my online school was booming – and did I mention I'm a mother of two boys (and two cats)? By midnight, my eyes were exhausted, my brain wanted to shut down, and my body was screaming for my bed. I wanted to keep writing, but physically and mentally I was spent. Suddenly, I felt this pull within my core. I leaned back in my chair and looked out of the window right next to me. To my surprise, I saw twinkling lights just on the other side of the glass. I instantly knew what they were: fireflies. There is very little green where I live, and after five years I have never seen fireflies dancing outside this window, which I've sat next to many, many times.

The pull in my core became a feeling of love running through me like a gentle hug. I remembered that, as a little girl, I had spent a lot of time enjoying nature, and that fireflies had been gems to my soul, treasures of the Earth. I knew this new appearance of them was a message, an attempt to share wisdom at a time when I needed it.

I later did some research and looked up the meaning of my message:

*'This spiritual totem's message dictates that we must be conscious, pay attention to intricacies, and exercise persistence if we wish to achieve success in our own lives. However [...] fireflies do not use heat to ignite their lights, symbolizing that we need not burn ourselves out in the pursuit of our goals.'*[1]

I read these words of wisdom, shut off my computer, and went to bed while thanking our Mother, Earth, for being there for me — I know that Mother Earth, who I chose to devote my life to, is the one who sent me the message. She does it all the time for me, through the mountains, trees, plants, animals, and sky. Don't dismiss her as your ancestor or guide, because she is probably one of the strongest spirits to yearn for your connection. In my opinion, all Witches should be connected to our Mother as much as they are to self. Our Mother, Earth, is the house you live in, the womb in which you're growing.

So practice being alert to messages, and notice not only the wisdom that comes to you directly, but the subtle signs as well. With time and patience, you'll build a strong, beautiful relationship with your ancestors, guides, and self.

---

1    www.sunsigns.org/firefly-animal-totem-symbolism-meanings/

# CLEANSING AND PROTECTING

Many of the people I meet seem to be carrying undesirable energies that don't belong to them. You can pick up others' negative energies or ill intents from just about anywhere — public transport, shops, sitting in traffic, restaurants, even social media. Do you regularly go out to bars, clubs, and big events? Then you're most definitely exposed to some major energy baggage.

What many don't realize is that these energies can affect your mood, thoughts, and actions, and ultimately disturb your life. Through my shop I come into contact with many people, and the majority are unnecessarily carrying energies of sadness, depression, worry, anger, fear, and so on. After these people leave the shop, their unwanted energies can linger on objects, products, plants, even my employees and me — the whole shop, in fact! So, a few times a day I perform a cleansing ritual in the shop; I also cleanse the customer before they leave. They always appreciate it and it makes my shop feel like a sanctuary.

Once you cleanse a space (*see below*), make sure you protect it from as many new negative energies as you can. Some will always get through, so regular cleansing is still important.

Cleansing and protecting can be very meditative. They also raise awareness, amplify inner senses, and are known to be healing too. You might also want to cleanse yourself if you feel unbalanced, emotional, unfocused, or uninspired. You may want to cleanse others too. Cleansing is a reset button for your energy.

I'm extremely sensitive to undesirable energies, and I take care of them straight away. I recommend you have a single daily ritual to banish such energies – a piece of wisdom every Witch should have under her Witchy hat.

## How to cleanse and protect

Here are my favorite ways to cleanse and protect which are both simple and effective.

### *Remove clutter and deep clean*

This is my No. 1 way to remove negative energy from any space, including your home. Tidy up and organize your possessions – even move furniture around – then give everything a thorough clean. Even just some good old soap and water will do the trick. Energies get stuck to furniture, objects, and even floors and ceilings. What's most important is to keep your home clean and organized.

## Create cleansing smoke

You can cleanse yourself and your space of unwanted energies by using the smoke of herbs, resin, or incense that have the properties to clear, cleanse, and banish. Some of my favorites are palo santo, yerba santa, rosemary, sandalwood, mugwort, dragon's blood, amber, cedar, myrrh, copal, and frankincense. If you're using loose herbs or incense, the most common way to burn them is to put a charcoal disc (you can buy these) at the bottom of a fireproof dish. Light the disc and place the herbs or incense on top to smolder gently. You can leave the bowl in the space you're working in, or walk round each room to allow the smoke to do its work everywhere. Always make sure you open at least one window or door to help unwanted energies leave the space and positive energies to flow in.

## Use spiritual sprays

Spiritual room sprays are a great alternative if you don't want smoke in your space (*see above*). I make them by combining the herbs or resins that have the desired properties with essential oils. They also smell lovely and my shop customers love them. You can make a room spray yourself using essential oils that help clear negative energy, such as sandalwood, lavender, frankincense, or patchouli. Mix them with water and a teaspoon of alcohol – I use vodka. You can spray the mist over yourself too.

### Place salt around the home

This is an easy and very effective method that I have used many times. Place bowls or open jars containing some salt in the corners of your home or space, even on top of your highest furniture or shelves. Leave the bowls out for about 24 hours, then remove them and get rid of the salt.

Salt naturally absorbs negative energy, so taking a bath with salt will also help to purify you. Dissolve two cups of sea salt or Himalayan salt in your bath – don't use table salt as this irritates the skin.

### Ring bells

The sound of bells or wind chimes in a Witch's home is a must. As the bells vibrate they shake the negative energies out of the space, then realign to create a flow of positive energy and revive your surroundings. You can also hang bells or wind chimes outside your house or on door handles. Ring a handbell on a daily basis, especially in spaces where you feel stagnant energy and where negative events, such as arguments, have taken place.

### Listen to music

Playing feel-good music that connects with you and moves you is great for keeping your energy at a high vibration and shaking off any negativity that has stuck to you. I particularly recommend high-vibration, uplifting music for clearing stagnant, old, or negative energies.

### Open windows

Fling open your curtains and windows, Witches! We're not vampires, you know! Let some light in; allow Mother Earth to bring you her healing. Let the breeze move across your house and keep your energies flowing beautifully.

### Turn to plants

Plants are Magickal. Not only do they have the power to purify the air, fill your home with our Mother's healing and love, and vibrate enchanting notes into your soul, they also keep negative energy away. They're natural protectors. Some of my favorite plants to keep in and around the home for protection and cleansing of negative energy are orchids, jasmine, cactus, spider plants, rosemary, basil, and rue.

### Let garlic protect you

Garlic has long been understood to have protective properties. Hang a bunch of garlic outside your door to keep away negative energies and unwanted spirits. Carry a clove in your purse or wallet (make sure to wrap it, perhaps in tin foil or some cloth). It repels thieves too. I put a garlic clove under my children's pillows to protect them from nightmares and unwanted spirits during the night. The plant rue is said to have a similar effect; carry it with you or plant it by the entrance to your home.

### Arrange crystals

Having protective crystals in your home and carrying or wearing them is a great way to aid protection and banish negative energy. You can place them anywhere and on anything, such as windowsills, coffee tables, and shelves, and in doorways. I even place crystals in my plants and under my bed. My very favorite crystals for protection include black tourmaline, smoky quartz, obsidian, turquoise, and labradorite.

### Create an energy shield

Each of us has the ability to create a personal energy shield. There are many ways to do this and many types of shield, but one of my favorite and easiest methods is for a light shield that is both protective and healing.

# Protection spell for creating a light shield

I create this shield for myself every morning before I get out of bed. It helps prevent evil and ill intent from affecting my energy, and brings strong healing powers by lifting my energy's vibration.

## What to do

◊ Find somewhere quiet and still to sit, then ground yourself (*see page 61*). Firmly plant your feet on the floor and take three deep breaths.

◊ Now visualize a ball of bright white light pulsating in your core, just behind your belly button. Imagine this light spreading throughout your entire body and filling every part of you. You're now a brilliant pulsating white light.

◊ With every breath you take, imagine this light expanding outward and forming a sphere with a thin, bluish outer layer, extending 4–5 feet (1.25–1.5 meters) around you — even under the ground beneath your feet.

◊ Sit within the sphere for a few more breaths and feel it vibrating all around you. Ask it to protect you from all negative energy, ill intent, evil, and anything that doesn't serve you well.

◊ When you feel ready, go on with your day and enjoy the benefits of your own inner power.

PART FOUR

# THE WITCH'S GARDEN OF HERBAL MAGICK

# INTRODUCTION TO THE WITCH'S GARDEN

A Witch's garden is her pride and joy, particularly the Magickal and medicinal herbs and flowers she grows there. As a child I was always curious about the herbs my mother used in her Magickal workings and natural remedies. She explained to me that each herb has its own unique properties in both medicine and Magick, and they all have the Earth's energy dwelling within them.

I've been working with herbal Magick since I was around five years old, at a time when I was suffering from nightmares. Spirits would visit me at night, and either surround me or sit by me. They didn't hurt me, but their presence was extremely intense and I found this very frightening. Every night when I started screaming my mother would cleanse the room, calm me down, and get a glass of water to which she added one or two bay leaves. She put this under my bed, the spirits vanished, and I instantly fell back to sleep. My mother eventually decided it was time I learnt to put the bay glass under my bed myself, and so began my use of herbal Magick.

Besides your own inner Magick, the most important ingredients of any spell or working are herbs, flowers, roots, and essential oils. It's easy to find information about them, and to familiarize yourself with their appearance and Magickal properties, but it's also important for you to build your own connection with them. Work with each one individually and spend time connecting to its specific energy, scent, and taste. Take your time and fill at least one page for each herb in your Book of Shadows, recording your experience of it.

The spells, potions, and other Magickal workings I share with you in this chapter all deal with herbal Magick and come from my Book of Shadows. I have either created them myself, received them from my elders and ancestors, or learnt them from spirits. I've chosen my favorites, which are simple yet powerful, and cover a wide range of uses from attracting love and healing a broken heart to purification and manifestation. I hope you'll find many you connect with and add to your own Book of Shadows.

In my spells I mention the words pinch and dash. This is my way of measuring the amount of a particular ingredient I wish to put into my Magickal workings. A dash is about half a teaspoon and a pinch is about a quarter of a teaspoon. I also use a tablespoon for some ingredients. Don't worry if you don't get the exact amount — use your intuition and the following recipes to guide you.

# ATTRACTING LOVE

These next few Magickal workings are for bringing love into your life. Love isn't something that can be manipulated or tampered with, however; these spells are not for making someone fall in love with you or for trapping them. They're for working with the universe to move things along faster or align you with love.

There are many different forms of love, but perhaps the most 'needed' are love from a partner or someone outside of self. Although this is an important and beautiful form of love, self-love should be the most important. These spells, or any love spell for that matter, can be directed at both forms. Set the focus on opening up to loving yourself, and connecting with yourself at a deeper level.

With all love I always heed warning, and ask for a love that is true, honest, and will serve all involved for the best. This helps to bring in true friends and partners who will cherish you for who you really are.

*Rosemary love oil*

Rosemary is infused with love properties, so even this simple love oil has great power to attract love into your life.

### What you need

A jar or bottle with a tightly fitting lid

Rosehip oil or extra virgin olive oil

3 sprigs rosemary

### What to do

◊ Fill the jar or bottle with the oil. Take the rosemary and into each sprig set an intention to do with love by saying what you desire, either aloud or in your head. For example, one of the sprigs could be for attracting love for self; another might be for attracting the right partner. As you set each intention, put the rosemary sprig into the oil.

◊ Seal the jar tightly then put it in a cool place away from direct light.

◊ The oil will work its Magick even if you leave the jar where it is, or you can use the Magick-infused oil to anoint candles, crystals, and tools for love purposes. When anointing, say aloud or in your head which of your three intentions you want to use.

# Cinnamon love-attracting sachet

Cinnamon is a powerful tool in Magick for attracting love. In this spell we're making a sachet that you can carry with you.

## What you need

A very small red bag or pouch

I cinnamon stick, snapped in half

½ teaspoon dried rose petals

½ teaspoon ground star anise

½ teaspoon dried basil

A small quartz crystal

## What to do

◊ Put all the ingredients into the bag. Wear this sachet around your neck or carry it in a pocket close to your heart. You can remove it at any time, but keep it close by.

## Bay leaf love-attracting spell

We all know that we can't force love — and nor should we dabble in Magick that aims to make someone fall in love with us. Instead, the purpose of this bay leaf love spell is to ignite love that is already there. It also helps to fire up love and passion in a relationship that needs a boost.

### What you need

A red-colored candle

Any love-spell oil, such as rosemary love oil
 (*see page 152*)

4 bay leaves

A small fireproof bowl

### What to do

◊ Anoint the candle with the love-spell oil, smoothing it onto the candle in a downward motion from top to bottom. Now light the candle.

◊ Sit quietly in front of the candle and gaze into its flame, clearing your mind of everything but thoughts of your lover. Think of the moments you were both happiest and most passionate, and of igniting that energy within your space.

◊ Now take a bay leaf, send those powerful thoughts into it, then hold it in the flame, dropping it into the bowl as soon as it ignites. Repeat the process, starting by gazing into the candle flame, three more times.

# HEALING A
# BROKEN HEART

Time heals a broken heart, but sometimes we need a little more than time to help us recover. These Magickal workings are meant to awaken the healing you have within you, especially when it comes to matters of the heart.

I want you to know that feeling pain, or feeling sad or broken, does not make you weak or mean that you *are* broken. Life comes with heartache, but I assure you that you're capable of healing. Take time for self-care and allow yourself extra compassion. Stay away from social media and allow yourself just to go through whatever emotions you're feeling instead of hiding them somewhere in the attic of your soul.

## Lemon balm broken-heart tea

My lemon balm tea for mending a broken heart works wonders for healing the heart and lifting the spirits. You can also drink the tea at any other time you feel vulnerable or need to calm your emotions.

### What you need

I tablespoon dried lemon balm

I teaspoon dried chamomile

I teaspoon dried lavender

I cup (250ml) water

### What to do

◊ Stir the herbs into the water and put the mixture in a small saucepan.

◊ Bring to the boil then simmer for 5 minutes.

◊ Allow the tea to cool a little, then strain to remove the herbs before drinking.

## Rose broken-heart potion

This potion is great for calming the nerves and sending away the hurt of a broken heart. It's especially effective at bedtime for calming the mind and heart from stress and worry, and aiding a peaceful night's sleep.

### What you need

A jar filled to three-quarters with grapeseed oil or extra virgin olive oil

1 pinch dried basil

2 tablespoons dried rose petals

Rose essential oil

Lavender essential oil

A rose quartz

### What to do

◊ Put the basil, rose petals, and essential oils into the jar of oil. Add the rose quartz and put the lid on the jar, or put the lid on and place the quartz on top.

◊ Take three deep breaths, then open the jar and rub some of the oil onto your wrist and over your heart.

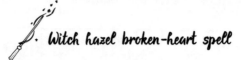

## Witch hazel broken-heart spell

I created this witch hazel broken-heart spell at the time I needed it most, and it's worked wonders every time I've cast it.

### What you need

A sheet of paper and a pen

1 teaspoon dried witch hazel

A quartz crystal

### What to do

◊ On the paper draw a heart about the size of your palm. In the heart write the word 'healing.' Place the witch hazel in the center of the heart and the quartz crystal on top of it.

◊ Place your right palm above the whole heart, not touching it but close enough to send in your energy. Now close your eyes and relax, then seal the spell by saying, 'My heart is healing, my heart is mending, it is not broken, this I say with love.' You can say something similar if your own words feel better for you.

◊ Keep your hand over the heart and repeat the enchantment twice more. You can keep the heart wherever you like. I like to keep it on my altar.

# PROTECTION

It's important to know how to protect yourself and your space. Many people go through life without clearing or protecting their energy, and they feel ill, stressed, depressed, tired, and, in many cases, lost. Life can become clouded and more difficult to navigate when you're carrying around energy that doesn't belong to you or negatively impacts your mind, body, and spirit. So get into the habit of adding protection into your life on a daily basis, and I assure you that things will start to shift in the most wonderful of ways!

Here are a few Magickal workings that are sure to bring protection into your life. You can use them for yourself or for loved ones, and for protection from negativity, intruders, ill will, misalignment, and more.

# Bay leaf banishing-night-spirits spell

This is the spell my mother used when I suffered nightmares as a child.

## What you need

I bay leaf

I glass cold water

½ teaspoon salt

## What to do

◊ Take the bay leaf and whisper into it 'May the spirits rest in peace so that I can also.'

◊ Put the bay leaf in the glass, add the salt then place the glass under the part of the bed you sleep in. The water is meant to expel any negative energy and the bay and salt provide protection against its return.

◊ In the morning pour away the water, then start over every night if necessary. I do this for my children and they sleep all the way through without any nightmares.

 *Rue protection sachet*

Rue has great protective qualities and I use it in most of my Magickal workings for protection. This sachet spell is simple and easy. Keep the sachet close to you at all times to dispel negativity and ill intent. You can also use it for protection while dreaming — simply place it under your pillow while you sleep.

### What you need

A small bag or pouch

1 tablespoon dried rue

1 tablespoon salt

1 tablespoon dried witch hazel

3 drops cedarwood essential oil or myrrh essential oil

### What to do

◊ Put all the ingredients, including the oil, into the bag.

◊ You can refresh your sachet with an extra drop of the essential oil it includes.

## Nettle uncrossing potion

Uncrossing is a term Witches often use for breaking, cutting, or undoing, and nettle is used to break a curse or jinx.

### What you need

A small bowl

1 tablespoon dried nettle

1 tablespoon dried agrimony

1 tablespoon sea salt

1 tablespoon charcoal crushed almost to a powder

4fl oz (120ml) safflower oil

### What to do

◊ In the bowl mix together the herbs, salt, and charcoal. Add the safflower oil until the mixture has the consistency of a facial scrub.

◊ Softly rub it onto your belly as you speak your intention. (Do a skin patch test first to check for any reaction.)

◊ Leave it there overnight but wash it off before the Sun rises. Repeat the process for two more days.

# Cumin thief-repellent spell

Since ancient times cumin has been known both for its healing properties and its ability to protect — including protection from any intruders with ill intentions.

### What you need

Ground cumin, dried basil, and salt in equal amounts (use tablespoons or cups)

### What to do

◊ Combine all the ingredients and either sprinkle the mixture around your home or in front of your house. I like to keep a sachet of this blend in the drawer where I keep my most sacred items.

# SUCCESS

Looking for more success in your life? If so, these Magickal workings are exactly what you need. Of course, success means something different to each person, so these spells are specifically designed to work with your personal desires. Success can take the form of a healthier you, a more peaceful home, an 'A' on your final exam, justice in a court case, or just about anything that you wish to go your way for the betterment of yourself or your life.

I love all the spells in this chapter, but my favorite go-to is the ginger root project-completion bath spell. I use it at least once a month, and it's helped me achieve tremendous success in all my projects. In fact, it's one of the spells I used to help me stay focused while working on this book and finish it on time. May all these spells bring you great success!

## Ginger root project-completion bath spell

Who doesn't need this spell? I often have more projects than I can handle at once, so I created this spell to help me to complete them all. It will calm your nerves, remove stress and anxiety, bring clarity to your task, and lift your spirits.

### What you need

A mixing bowl

1 cup (300g) Epsom salts

1 cup (300g) pink Himalayan salt

2 tablespoons dried chopped ginger root

1 tablespoon dried juniper leaf

10 drops copal essential oil

10 drops ylang ylang essential oil

### What to do

◊ Combine all the ingredients in the bowl.

◊ Add 1 cup (300g) of this blend to your bath before you start work on your project.

## Nutmeg career-success incense

You can use this incense at home while getting ready for work, while working at home, or before an important meeting. It invites the winds of the Earth to push you high into the position you want, or to achieve all that you wish for in your career. And just wait until you feel what it does to your energy!

### What you need

A small bowl

A jar with a tightly fitting lid

2 tablespoons of ground nutmeg

1 tablespoon myrrh resin

1 tablespoon dragon's blood resin or powder

1 tablespoon basil

1 tablespoon dried yarrow

11 drops of benzoin essential oil

### What to do

◊ Combine all the ingredients in the bowl, then put the mixture in the jar to use when you need it.

◊ To use, burn a dash of this blend in a fireproof bowl or by another method you prefer.

## Rosehip relationship-success ice cube

An ice cube spell? Yes, that's right. I thought of this when it was about 100°F (38°C) outside and I was holding an ice cube to my chest to cool myself down while a friend was lamenting that there was no longer any passion in her relationship. As she was talking, my ice cube suddenly escaped my fingers. As it fell to the ground I had flashes of myself preparing this spell to refuel a relationship. When I got home I meditated on the experience and created the following spell to bring your desires to your relationship. It's best worked in hot weather, and you'll need to wait for a Waxing Moon phase (*see pages 89–90*) to perform it.

### What you need

A bowl

1 cup (250ml) olive oil

2 tablespoons dried rosehip

1 tablespoon fenugreek

1 tablespoon crushed cinnamon stick

1 tablespoon rosemary

Peel of 1 orange, chopped

An ice-cube tray

### What to do

◊ In the bowl combine all the ingredients, then fill the ice-cube tray with the mixture and freeze it.

◊ After sunset during a Waxing Moon phase, pour yourself a glass of red wine, take the tray of ice cubes, and sit outside to enjoy the night, even if the sky is cloudy. If you don't drink alcohol, a strawberry, pomegranate, or cherry drink will do as well.

◊ Take one of the ice cubes and hold it in your fingers while you take a sip of your drink. Now lick the ice cube once and whisper into it one thing you wish to bring into your relationship. Then gently drop the cube onto the ground to symbolize melting the ice between you and your lover.

◊ Make as many wishes as you like, using a new cube for each one. Discard the cubes you don't need.

# WEALTH AND ABUNDANCE

Money is vital for survival in the modern world. We have bills to pay and we want money to spend on things we enjoy. These Magickal workings help to draw in wealth and abundance. They're simple but powerful, and if cast correctly you'll soon have prosperity in your life.

As with all things, wealth and abundance mean different things to different people. For me, they mean being able to keep a roof over my head, put food on the table, and not having to struggle. I also appreciate what I have. There is nothing wrong with wanting more money to flow into your life or more abundance to be present. You deserve it! Just be conscious of what you're asking for and start with reasonable desires — a raise, a new job opportunity, or money owed showing up. Start there and always remember to be grateful for whatever comes into your life.

## Bayberry blank-check money spell

I have come across various versions of blank-check spells and I still come back to this bayberry version I learnt from a spirit I met on my porch, who told me a little trick that I have found particularly successful. This is the spell I'm sharing here.

### What you need

Your checkbook

A jar of water

1fl oz (30ml) bayberry oil

¼ teaspoon cinnamon

### What to do

◊ When it's a Full Moon phase, take a blank check from your checkbook and write 'Now' on the 'date' line. On the 'Pay to' line write your full name. In the box where you usually write the amount in figures write 'What is owed,' and do the same on the line where you usually write the amount in words. Sign the check in your usual way.

◊ Put the check into the jar of water, along with the bayberry oil and the cinnamon. Now spit once into the jar, screw on the lid, and wait for money to come into your life.

## Allspice money rice spell

The enchanted rice in this spell isn't for eating, but it still packs a punch — by bringing in money when you need it.

### What you need

A small bowl

A jar with a tightly fitting lid

1 cup (200g) brown rice

2 tablespoons ground allspice

1 tablespoon black pepper powder

1 tablespoon dried dill

1 tablespoon ground nutmeg

1fl oz (30ml) verbena essential oil

A low-denomination bill

Clear quartz chippings

1 tablespoon cinnamon

### What to do

◊ Mix all of the edible ingredients, plus the verbena oil, in the bowl.

◊ Cut the bill into little pieces and combine with the other ingredients. Take the quartz chippings and stir them in too.

◊ Put the mixture into the jar and screw on the lid. Sprinkle the cinnamon on the top of the lid or around the jar, or both.

◊ Place the jar in the location you need money, such as at home or at your workplace.

## Alfalfa buried-apple spell

This spell sends a message to the Elements that you desire money, wealth, or another form of abundance, such as a new opportunity. You must create the spell at night during a Full Moon phase and have easy access to a natural environment.

### What you need

I green apple

I teaspoon dried alfalfa leaf

I teaspoon dried chamomile

I teaspoon dried chopped ginger root

2 or 3 bay leaves

I tablespoon honey

### What to do

◊ Using a sharp knife, carefully carve a tunnel-like hole in the side of the apple, stopping when you reach the core.

◊ Stuff the alfalfa, chamomile, ginger, and honey into the hole then press the bay leaf in to act as a seal — it will look as though the apple is growing bay out of its side.

◊ During a Full Moon phase, bury the apple at midnight in a natural environment.

# LUCK

Luck isn't something that comes easily. You have to hone its energy and make it yours. Lady Luck prefers those who call upon her spirit, and these Magickal workings do just that.

Luck spells have always been extremely popular. People want to win at everything, they want to believe that they can make the right the decisions, choose the right answers, and be the chosen one, so to speak. Here's the thing: luck is very real, but it's a form of attraction mixed with work. There is always work to be done. Things don't just happen by luck, but a luck spell can most definitely help to make happen whatever it is you're working on. Luck spells are like the icing on the cake — they add that extra something to bring it all together. So indulge in these fantastic spells and I hope they bring you what you seek.

## High John the Conqueror luck oil

Both thyme and High John the Conqueror have properties for bringing luck into one's life. Carry this oil with you whenever you need extra luck, such as for a job interview or a first date.

### What you need

A vial or very small jar that you can carry around with you

Extra virgin olive oil (enough to fill your vial or jar by three-quarters)

1 teaspoon thyme

1 teaspoon ground High John the Conqueror root

### What to do

◊ Fill your vial or jar with the oil and add the thyme and High John the Conqueror root.

◊ Keep the vial close to you whenever it's important that things go your way.

The same oil made only with High John the Conqueror root can also be used for anointing candles. For this I make greater quantities than for the vial, and grate whole High John the Conqueror root instead of using ground. I then leave the oil to infuse for at least one lunar cycle before using it for anointing.

# Patchouli luck perfume

Bring in luck by wearing this powerful Magickal perfume.

## What you need

A vial

Enough jojoba oil to fill your vial by three-quarters

7 drops patchouli essential oil

4 drops cedarwood essential oil

2 drops lavender essential oil

2 drops ylang ylang essential oil

1 drop myrrh essential oil

A citrine crystal

## What to do

◊ Pour the jojoba oil into the vial and add the essential oils.

◊ Seal the vial, shake well, and leave for three days in a cool, dark place with the citrine crystal next to it to add some oomph to the blend.

◊ When the perfume is ready to use, place a couple drops on the back of your neck, behind your ears and on the back of your wrists. (Do a skin patch test first to check for any skin irritation.)

 Fennel luck charm-bag

Many people like wearing or carrying a charm for luck, and this fennel luck charm-bag will not disappoint. To break a streak of bad luck, carry the charm-bag with you for seven days.

## What you need

A small green or yellow bag or pouch

1 tablespoon fennel seeds

1 teaspoon dried basil

1 teaspoon dried bergamot

1 teaspoon dried chopped ginger root

3 cloves

1 citrine or a few citrine chippings

A strand of your hair or a few of your nail clippings

## What to do

◊ Put all the ingredients into the bag. It's now ready for immediate use!

# HEALING

Being mindful of self and taking great care of your physical self is key to being the best you. Healing spells are great for aiding discomfort and getting rid of what doesn't serve you physically, mentally, or spiritually.

I believe healing spells are an act of self-love; anything that works to bring you back to center and rid you of what doesn't serve you is an act of love unto oneself. You can use the spells in the following pages for yourself or for loved ones. They're also great to help amplify your innate healing ability. These are some of my easiest healing workings, but they won't let you down. They are potent and do their work incredibly well.

## Catnip healing spell

This spell uses candle anointment to bring all-round healing.

### What you need

A blue candle

2 teaspoons dried catnip

1 teaspoon dried coltsfoot

1 teaspoon dried comfrey

1fl oz (30ml) sandalwood essential oil

### What to do

◊ Take your candle. If you're performing this spell for someone else, carve their name on it.

◊ Mix together the herbs and oil.

◊ Smooth the oil mixture over the candle in a downward motion, top to bottom. This motion brings in what you're asking for.

◊ As you anoint the candle, say your intent, such as 'Bring me healing, bring me strength, I call on divine Magick with this breath.' (You can adapt the words if you wish, and should if the spell is for another person.)

◊ Now light the candle and let it burn all the way to the bottom.

# Garlic foot-soak healing potion

Garlic has long been used in Magickal workings. It's a potent and Magickal bulb that should be a staple in your home — my family uses it almost daily for spells and remedies, and in cooking. The amount of garlic in this healing potion means your feet won't smell pretty, but it will draw out illness and pull in healing.

## What you need

A small saucepan

2 cups (500ml) water

1 tablespoon dried coltsfoot

1 tablespoon dried St John's wort

1 tablespoon dried wormwood

1 tablespoon birch bark

4 cloves garlic, crushed

1fl oz (30ml) oregano oil

A bucket or large bowl, half filled with cold water, in which to place your feet

## What to do

◊ Bring the 2 cups of water to the boil in a small saucepan, then add all other ingredients and simmer for 5–7 minutes.

◊ Let the mixture cool a little, then pour the entire contents of the saucepan into the bucket of water.

◊ Now take the bucket into a quiet room and turn off the lights (or dim them). If you like, light some incense of your choice and play soft, meditative music to create a calming and healing environment.

◊ Check the temperature of the water: it should be tepid or cool. Immerse your feet in the water and close your eyes. Soak your feet for 10–15 minutes.

◊ Repeat once a day for three days in a row.

## Tobacco banishing-illness incense

This incense aims to cure sickness in the home; it can also alleviate sadness at home – if someone has died, for example. It also purifies and protects against negative spirits. This incense is so powerful that you can feel it working even before you burn it.

### What you need

I tobacco leaf or I tablespoon loose tobacco

I tablespoon dried basil

I tablespoon ground cloves

I tablespoon copal resin

I teaspoon myrrh resin

I teaspoon ground cinnamon

¼ teaspoon mugwort

2 slices dried orange

I slice dried lemon

A jar with a tightly fitting lid

### What to do

◊ Crush all the ingredients together and make sure they're thoroughly mixed.

◊ Burn a small amount of the incense to release its healing powers. Store the rest in a jar for future use.

# PURIFICATION

Purification has long been a staple in my family. We purify everything from new objects brought into the home to anyone needing a clearing of bad energy or curse. Purification clears and removes unwanted energy and brings in positive and peaceful energies.

It's important to purify your tools, altars, sacred spaces, and, of course, yourself, from time to time. Since I practice Magickal workings daily and work as a healer, I make sure to purify myself every day.

I've included my go-to methods in the following pages. They're just lovely and work beautifully.

# Basil purification spray

Basil is a giant in Magick, and has many different uses. This simple spray can be used to purify and spiritually cleanse sacred objects, spaces, altars, and any other part of the home that you feel needs ridding of stagnant energy. The scent alone is uplifting and Magickal, and this spray is sure to become one of your favorite ways to use the power of basil.

## What you need

16fl oz (450ml) water

1 lemon, cut in half

A small handful of basil leaves

1 tablespoon thyme

An empty spray bottle

## What to do

◊ Bring the water to the boil in a saucepan, add the lemon halves, basil, and thyme, then simmer for 10 minutes.

◊ Leave to cool, then strain to remove the herbs and lemon. Pour into a spray bottle and it's ready to use.

#  Thyme loose purification incense

Not only does this purification incense smell like heaven, it's also a great way to purify and cleanse both objects and spaces of negative energy. Use it after any Magickal work or when you need to move the energy around the home.

## What you need

2 teaspoons thyme

1 teaspoon rosemary

1 teaspoon green or purple sage

1 teaspoon ground star anise

2 drops thyme essential oil

1 drop lavender essential oil

A small jar with a tightly fitting lid

## What to do

◊ Grind the thyme, rosemary, and sage together as finely as possible.

◊ Now stir in the star anise powder and the essential oils, and put the mixture in the jar.

◊ Use a pinch of the mixture to burn as a loose incense.

## Lavender purification bath salt

Need to clear away the stresses of the day and indulge in a divine bath? This lavender purification bath salt is for you! Not only does it relax the nerves, calm the mind, and embrace the skin, it also clears away any energy that doesn't belong to you and any energy that is negative or harmful.

### What you need

I cup (300g) sea salt

2 tablespoons dried lavender

I tablespoon rosemary

I teaspoon dried peppermint leaves

4 drops lavender essential oil

2 drops frankincense essential oil

### What to do

◊ Mix all the ingredients together, then stir about 3 tablespoons of the mixture into your bath before you get in.

# New Beginnings

Spells for new beginnings can help you restart, reset, and open new paths for yourself. New beginnings can seem scary; we're wired for comfort after all, and even when comfort is painful, we sometimes accept it because we're used to it or believe it's what we deserve. However, you, my dear, are precious, and you deserve to live a precious life. It isn't always going to be perfect, but it can be a lot easier than it is now. Life can be whatever you want it to be, and feel how you want it to feel (or at least feel close to that desire).

I love new beginnings. They're a reset button, a fresh start, a do over, a chance to try again with something that isn't working. New beginnings are everyone's birthright. So here are some Magickal workings that are all simple yet effective and will help you to start anew.

## Lotus New Moon energy oil

This spell moves old energy out of a room and replaces it with new energy. It's great for those who have recently finished a relationship, a job, or a friendship, or who have suffered the death of someone living with them. This oil can also be used for anointing candles, tools, and crystals for use in other spells with the same purpose.

### What you need

A mixing bowl

1 cup (250ml) safflower oil

2 tablespoons dried blue lotus flower

1 tablespoon dried chopped birch bark

1 tablespoon dried elderberries

1 tablespoon dried white horehound

A jar with a tightly fitting lid

### What to do

◊ Before you make the oil, open at least one window in the room you're working in to allow old energies to move out and new ones to come in. If possible, open a window in every room of the house, even in a hallway or staircase.

◊ In the bowl combine all the ingredients, then put the mixture in the jar.

◊ Pour some of the oil into the palm of your hand and rub your hands together quickly to raise the energy.

◊ Stand in the middle of the room, ground yourself (*see page 61*), and focus on your intent.

◊ Now, with lots of energy and exaggerated movements, clap your hands three times, each time saying out aloud, 'Out with the old and in with the new.'

◊ The shift in the air will happen immediately. If you're sensitive to feeling beyond our Earthly realm you'll feel the peace flowing into your home or space.

◊ When you've finished the spell, replace the lid on the jar and store the mixture until you next use it.

## Wood betony new-beginnings foot oil

This oil aims to imbue the feet with inspiration to move forward, breaking the chains from them so that you can walk freely again. It's also great for anointing candles, crystals, and tools for similar spells. You'll need to wait for a New Moon before you can actually use the oil.

### What you need

A mixing bowl

1 cup (250ml) grapeseed oil

2 tablespoons dried wood betony

1 tablespoon dried yarrow

1 tablespoon dried blessed thistle

Enough plantain leaves to wrap around your feet

### What to do

◊ In the bowl combine the oil and herbs.

◊ During a New Moon phase, rub the oil all over your feet and wrap them in the plantain leaves. Let them soak for 20 minutes so that the oil can work its Magick, then remove and discard the leaves.

## Ashwagandha cacao drink

Think of this drink as a Magickal hot chocolate. It allows your presence to move in different energy levels, conjuring winds to push and guide you to new beginnings and new journeys.

### What you need

A mixing bowl

2 teaspoons dried ashwagandha

½ cup (70g) raw cacao powder

1 tablespoon dried shatavari

½ teaspoon vanilla extract

1 whole star anise

½ teaspoon ground cinnamon

½ teaspoon ground cardamom

½ teaspoon pink Himalayan salt

A jar with a tightly fitting lid

1 cup (250ml) milk (preferably plant-based, such as oat or almond)

### What to do

◊ Mix the dry ingredients together in the bowl. Put the mixture in the jar and screw on the lid.

◊ In a small saucepan bring the milk to the boil. Add
   1 tablespoon of the mixture to the milk, then stir
   and simmer for 3 minutes. Allow the drink to cool a
   little, stir in sugar, maple syrup or agave nectar to add
   sweetness if you wish, then enjoy!

◊ Keep the mixture in the jar until you next want to
   perform this spell.

# PSYCHIC
# ENHANCEMENT

Take your gifts to another level with these methods for enhancing psychic abilities. They're meant to amplify your inner Magick and tap into your consciousness. These are perfect to cast before you start to meditate and before bedtime when you're more open to inner connection.

I believe we all have gifts within us. Some of us are born with them, others recognize they have a gift but need to develop it, while others haven't yet experienced their gifts. This is all perfectly okay, and there are many factors that play a role in how fast we build our skills.

Practice is key! Just like any other muscle in our body, we need to work our psychic muscles to develop them. The methods in the follow pages will surely get you feeling like you belong in the cast of *Practical Magic*!

# Star anise psychic-amplifier and protection incense

When I was growing up star anise was a staple both in our kitchen and in our Magickal workings, and I still use it often today. Not only does the incense here smell like a dream but it's powerful, too, helping to heighten psychic ability and at the same time providing psychic protection from negative energies.

Use a small amount of the blend to burn as a loose incense, or just add ground star anise to myrrh or copal resin and burn the mixture while meditating or performing Magickal work.

## What you need

1–3 whole star anise

1 tablespoon copal resin

1 tablespoon myrrh resin

## What to do

◊ Crush the ingredients together and make sure they're thoroughly mixed.

◊ Burn as you would any other resin.

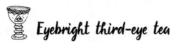 ## Eyebright third-eye tea

I love teas, whether creating them or sipping their enchanting waters. This eyebright third-eye tea is ideal for taking before divination, meditation, or other spell work. This recipe makes enough for one cup.

### What you need

I cup (250ml) water

I tablespoon dried eyebright

I teaspoon dried passionflower

I whole star anise

I teaspoon dried rose petals

### What to do

◊ Put the ingredients in a small saucepan, bring to the boil, and then simmer for 5–7 minutes. Alternatively, leave to steep in a teapot of freshly boiled water for 8–10 minutes.

◊ Set aside the tea until cool enough to drink.

# Lemongrass intuition-amplifier wash

Use this mixture to wash your altar, Magickal tools, and home; it will heighten your intuition and bring protection against negative energies. Note that this wash is not to be consumed.

## What you need

3 cups (750ml) water (preferably rainwater)

1 tablespoon dried lemongrass

3 bay leaves

2 teaspoons dried jasmine

2 teaspoons dried catnip

2 teaspoons dried wormwood

Half a lemon

## What to do

◊ Put all the ingredients in a small saucepan, bring to the boil, then simmer for 5 minutes.

◊ Let the mixture cool and then strain it so that you're left only with the liquid wash. This is now ready for use.

# MANIFESTATION

Modern-day Witchery is all about manifesting; Witches are focused on creating the lives they want. These spells will not disappoint, and will move mountains for the desires you hold.

As I've mentioned previously, manifesting has a lot to do with your Magickal attitude and that you need to feel as though you already have what it is you want. You must feel it, see it, and dream it for its energy to have presence in your life, and in turn it will attract those things you want straight to you. It really isn't that complicated, and the manifesting spells in the following pages will be sure to help you manifest your deepest desires.

## Wheat manifesting mail spell

This manifesting spell is dear to my heart. I discovered it in a vision in my sleep, during which I performed it as though I'd done it a million times before. I wrote it down the second I woke up. I can't speak highly enough of this spell; it's come good many times over.

### What you need

Paper for letter-writing

A red pen or a quill with menstrual blood for ink

A stem of wheat

### What to do

◊ Write a letter to the universe, perhaps to 'Dear Spirit' or to a deity or similar of your choice, expressing what you need. Include plenty of detail. For instance, when I wanted a car, I included the number of seats, the color, and so on.

◊ At the end of the letter write something along the lines of 'P.S. Although these are my exact desires, I'm open to what you know will serve me best — as long as you bring me a car.' This leaves open the possibility of manifesting not just the car you've asked for, but an even better one. Bear in mind that by only giving the powers that be permission to bring what was asked for, it can take much longer and may not happen at all.

◊ Sign the letter, fold it twice toward you, then place it in an envelope large enough to fit without further folding, along with the wheat stem (if necessary, bend this to fit it in). Seal the envelope and mail it to yourself. When the letter comes back, place it on your altar.

## Bergamot manifesting room spray

Use this spray around the room where you're practicing manifesting Magick. You can also use it when you meditate — it relaxes the mind and lifts the spirits, enhancing spiritual connection. It also smells amazing.

### What you need

A 2fl oz (60ml) spray bottle

11 drops bergamot essential oil

7 drops chamomile essential oil

7 drops lavender essential oil

### What to do

◊ Put the oils in the bottle and fill to the top with water.

◊ Put on the lid and shake well before every use.

# Spearmint Moon-water manifesting tea

I created this spell after months of trying to get Moon-water to work in manifesting, and eventually succeeded with this Magickal tea. You must only perform it during a Full Moon phase (*see page 91*).

## What you need

A 24fl oz (700ml) jar

Clean rainwater or tap water

11 spearmint leaves

1 pinch dried cilantro (coriander)

Crystal quartz chippings

1 bay leaf

6 lemon slices

Honey, to taste

## What to do

◊ Fill the jar with rainwater (or tap water if you live in the city or another area with high pollution). Put the mint into the jar followed by the cilantro and quartz.

◊ Hold the bay leaf against your lips, take three deep breaths, and each time you exhale slowly blow your Magick into the leaf while visualizing what you wish to manifest. Now add the bay leaf to the jar and screw on the lid.

◊ Leave the jar anywhere, indoors or outdoors, where it will be exposed to the Full Moon; even if it's cloudy, the water will still absorb the Moon's delicious energies.

◊ Return to the jar before the Sun rises, and move it so that it will be protected from daylight.

◊ When you're ready, add the lemon slices to the jar, replace the lid, and place your hands on the jar while you meditate. As you meditate, use a chant of repeated words to help manifest what you wish for. Do this for at least 10 minutes so that the water becomes infused with your wishes.

◊ Your Moon-water tea is now ready to do its work. Boil 1 cup of the tea, straining the liquid as you pour it out if you wish. Add a touch of honey and let the tea cool a little, then relax somewhere quiet and enjoy drinking your Magick. Perhaps light some incense to enhance the Magickal energies.

◊ Save the rest of the Moon-water in the fridge and drink the infusion hot every day until it's used up.

≺≺❧

I hope these spells, potions, and other Magickal workings are of great use to you. Feel free to adjust them according to your intuition, and continue to practice your own spells as well as the ones I share with you here. Remember to keep a record of the outcomes in your Book of Shadows.

# CREATING YOUR OWN SPELLS

Why would you want to create your own spells when there are a gazillion spells already out there? Well, for starters, they're not yours. They don't carry as much power as they would if you created them yourself. Your own spell will be infused with something nobody else's spell has: your own inner Magick! Your own thoughts, feelings, energy, intuition, intentions, and your very essence go into every spell you create yourself. That makes for some pretty powerful Magick.

Creating a spell is like baking a delicious cake — you get to choose the ingredients based on the outcome you want. On your first attempt it may not metaphorically look or taste exactly the way you hoped, but with lots of practice you'll get the result you want.

Here is a guide to the steps involved when crafting a spell. Eventually this process will become as natural to you as breathing.

### Think about the aim of your spell

Be clear about the intention of your spell from the start. What do you wish to accomplish with it? As a novice, stick to just one intent for each spell and try to be specific. If it's a spell for protection, what kind of protection? Where is this protection needed? Who is the protection for? And so on. Write everything down and keep breaking it open until you feel you've reached the clearest intent for the spell.

### Gather your tools and ingredients

Here's the fun part! Begin to think about and collect the ingredients, tools, and any other items you'll need to create your spell. Think of the Elements you wish to include, and the correspondences. Your spell doesn't need to be extravagant or involve a ton of ingredients or tools. It's best to keep it simple, and focus on the things that will work best to manifest the intent of the spell.

### Write down your spell

It's time for you to write your spell! You may want to cast your spell during a certain phase of the Moon, or a particular day of the week or special time, so consider this before you start writing. If you want to use words with your spell, either out loud or in your head, start with something simple; don't go too fancy at this point. After you've practiced your spell and memorized what you want to say, you can, if you wish, adapt the words so that they rhyme — I call this poetic tongue. This makes the spell easier to remember and raises more energy.

I myself don't write words to go with my spells as I've always been able to cast them by speaking only with my energy. This requires extreme focus and you need to be in full control of the emotions, feelings, and energies within and surrounding you. Even so, I always write down my spells in my Witch's Journal, so I have a record of the process even if it doesn't involve any words.

Take time to memorize the process of your spell, too, including the items needed and what to do with them. In doing so you add spirit to the spell because you're internalizing it. You'll then have it living within you, and there is nothing more powerful than that.

## Prepare your space and yourself

Now that you've created your spell, it's time to get ready to cast it. Find a space that is completely quiet and where you won't be disturbed. Light candles and burn herbs, resin, or incense to establish a spell-casting space. Use whatever colors and scents connect with you at this moment to help you focus. Cleanse yourself and your space (*see page 138*), then sit down on a chair or the floor and ground yourself (*see page 61*). Allow your mind to come to a place of stillness. You want to remove all outside influences and noise before starting.

### Do Magick!

When you're ready, raise energy for your spell (*see page 67*) and spill your Magick with confidence – pour your soul into it! Be mindful of practices such as raising energy and grounding, and reapply them during the casting process if necessary.

When you're done with your Magickal workings dispose of materials, such as your burnt herbs and candles, by burying them in dirt. Cleanse the space, yourself, and all the tools you used.

Store your tools in a dedicated area – this can be anything from a tiny corner of your dresser to a full table. When I was younger and in college I kept my tools in a chest under my bed. Anywhere is fine – just make sure to keep it clean and clear of stagnant energy.

### Learn from your experience

Make sure you take notes on how the spell-casting went. Write them in your Grimoire if you've started one. Take note of the feelings, energies, pulls and pushes, messages if any came, and how your body felt and reacted, and so on. Remember that many spells don't work right away. They take time to manifest, especially for new Witches, as it takes time to build your power to its highest potential. It might be a week, or even a month, before you observe any changes or shifts. Also, the greater the spell's purpose, the more time it may take to manifest, so take that into account.

There is and always will be practice involved in our craft, and this speaks loudly when it comes to spell-casting. Work no more than one spell a week, because a key part of casting spells is observation and taking note of the outcome so you can go back and make adjustments. You need time to do this before embarking on a new spell.

# 'WHY AREN'T MY SPELLS WORKING?'

This is the question I'm asked most frequently, and is usually followed by 'Where did I make a mistake?' I don't consider there to be any 'mistakes' in Magick because there really isn't any right or wrong way to practice. It's just a case of making adjustments.

Working with Magick involves chemistry, astrology, and a spiritual essence, and to wield our craft successfully we need to meet somewhere in the middle of all three. But the most important ingredient that goes into a spell is you. The mind is a cauldron, and each thing you put into it becomes part of the recipe of the Magick you're working. Make sure to be mindful of what needs to go into the recipe to get it just right.

The following is a basic checklist of ways to give yourself the best chance of success with your Magick.

## Make your intents clear

From the start, be really clear about what it is you want to manifest, otherwise the message is scrambled before it even leaves you. Being unclear results in things taking longer, and often they don't happen at all. If you cast a spell to manifest a new job, be specific about what kind of job you want – what the position entails, what kind of money you want to make, and so on. If you're unclear about what you're asking for, you may just get random job opportunities that you don't want, or not get any at all. It's all in the detail.

## Believe in yourself

To give your intents the power they need to manifest, you must believe in them and in your craft. It's vital that you have confidence in what your Magick can achieve. For instance, if you cast a money spell asking for a thousand dollars before the end of the week, you have to believe it can happen, and also that you already have that money. If you don't believe it can happen, then it won't.

When I was in my twenties I devoted a lot of my time to practicing money spells, and by my thirties I had mastered them: I always have enough money to pay my bills, to enjoy life, to run my business, and to donate to charities. The first step is to think where this money is going to come from. If you're a business owner, perhaps you want to direct this spell to bring money through your business; if you have money owed to you, then direct it there. If you don't know where the money could come from, be open to the possibility of it coming in from anywhere.

## Be positive

When working spells and setting goals or intents, it's important that you do so from a place of confidence and power. You need to feel calm and still. Feelings of worry, panic, or neediness will only interfere with your Magick. You have to feel the Magick in your soul and believe it's already with you.

Envisage yourself with the thing you desire. How does it look, feel, and taste? Think about every detail. For instance, if you desire love and you cast a spell for attracting love, you need to come from a place of love. Feelings of being unloved or alone will prevent a love spell from having any effect. So before casting this spell, transport yourself back to a time when you felt loved, or imagine being in love. How does it make you feel to have someone love you? Think about how your smile lights up, and what your body feels like. You need to become what it is you want to attract.

## Have patience

Hurried or stressful energies mean that intents take longer to manifest, and they also interfere with the message you're trying to send out. Magick takes time, so be patient. When I cast my spells I like to let them just be, rather than worrying all the time about whether they're working. I know that they'll come good when the time is right.

## Focus on one thing at a time

Give your full attention to just one of the things you wish to manifest. Nurture it and put all of your energy into this one thing. Achieving multiple Magickal intents at the same time takes many years of practice; until then, working on more than one intent at a time will most likely mean they interfere with one another. Baby steps, dear Witches. So work on one spell at a time, and give each one your full attention. Once it's done, you can move on to another.

## Trust in destiny

Your intents will manifest only if they're of benefit to you. Your ancestors and guides will not allow something that will not serve you well. Trust them, trust your journey, and trust the universe. Perhaps you're not yet ready for what you want — but it may show up when you are. For example, when I first wanted to publish a book, I worked hard on this intention for months but it just didn't show up. Instead, it showed up when I was ready; when I was further along on my spiritual journey and knew without question what my contribution to this planet would be.

I never lost faith in becoming an author. I went forward and worked on self, and you're right now reading the result of that journey.

I revel in a place of delicious synchronicities. My lips spill spells with grace and my presence embodies the presence of my Magick. It didn't always feel this way, and there are times when I still have to work extra hard to see the fruits of my Magickal labors. Practicing Magick is just that: practice. When we accept this, everything starts to come together. Magick should be fun, a beautiful mystery you welcome into your life. Allow yourself to be as enchanted by your journey as by your Magick, and travel through a world of limitless possibilities. You're Magickal. Don't ever forget that.

# PART FIVE

# PRACTICE RESPONSIBLY

# 10 Ways to Heal the Earth

Now, more than ever, the Witch within you needs you to wake up to help protect the Earth — our Mother, our home. Without our collective awakening the Earth cannot be healed. It doesn't matter how much or how little you do, as long as you do something to help heal and protect our planet, our Mother, from dying of the injustices she suffers in the world today. We all are children of the Earth, and we have a responsibility to return her love and keep her safe. I'm not trying to be dramatic here — I'm actually *being* dramatic. Witches, you're waking and remembering our purpose, our calling, here on Earth and it's time to answer the cry for help from our Mother that we feel within our bones.

Find the time in your life to be active in making a difference to the health of our Mother. There are many small changes we can all make in our everyday lives, and also ways that we Witches can protect other Mother's health when we carry out our Magickal workings. Here are just a few:

1. Reuse jars for new Magickal workings or for other purposes around the home. Pull-out candle jars can be used for storage or as vases.

2. Collect rainwater for use in Magickal workings and for your garden.

3. Use recycled paper.

4. Choose matches over lighters.

5. Spend time in nature, and let her know how much you love and appreciate her.

6. Use natural cleaning products in your home.

7. Air-dry your laundry when possible.

8. Stay informed about the state of the Earth.

9. Invest your money in environmentally and socially conscious businesses.

10. Use your Magick for healing our Mother.

You can also visit my website (www.novembersage.com) to find out more about The Witch's Purpose Organization, a non-profit I founded for those wishing to be actively involved in healing and protecting our Mother and all of her children.

# INTEGRITY IN WITCHERY

Among the issues that affect the modern Witch is that of cultural appropriation — when a dominant culture copies traditions of a minority culture. This has become hugely important to the Witch community, where truth and integrity are everything. With so much false information about what it means to be a Witch, many people are using elements of others cultures without even realizing it.

For instance, using herbal smoke or incense to cleanse is an ancient tradition that occurs in many cultures, including the Witch community. I prefer to use the term 'cleansing' rather than 'smudging' as the latter is a practice specific to Native American culture. I would also suggest avoiding the use of white sage for cleansing, as I understand it to be currently endangered, but other types of sage work equally well, as do cedar, juniper, and rosemary, or you can use resins, such as frankincense or copal.

Other examples of practices and expressions that in my opinion should not be used outside their traditional culture include the Native American 'spirit animal'; instead I suggest you refer to a 'spirit guide.' Additionally, instead of 'chakras' use 'energy points', and leave 'mantra' for Hindus and instead use 'chant.'

There are so many examples that I suggest you do your own research and ask yourself, Am I doing this because it's a trend, or is it out of genuine interest? There is so much information about this subject, so dive in and learn how to avoid cultural appropriation. Even when writing this book I avoided using certain words used only by practicing Witches, and chose alternatives instead. It all comes down to respect for other cultures and thinking about what's okay and what's not. Everyone has a choice. I hope you choose to be mindful and respectful of others' feelings.

## The bigger picture

I'm hopeful for the day when we can peacefully co-exist and all that we see is the soul of everything and everyone — not race, color, gender, shape, religion, or other sacred practice. Regardless of how you feel about politics and who is in office, you have a voice and it should be heard. Get involved and really put steps in place to make a difference. For instance, I decided to run for public office on the environmental platform, something I would once never have imagined myself doing – and you can do it too, dear Witches!

Find out about your local elected officials and what they do – and talk to them. They're there to listen to you; it's part of their job. You have a voice and it matters. Think of the issues that mean the most to you, such as immigration, education, mental health, equality and rights, climate change, and so on. Speak up and state your concerns and ideas, but stay calm, patient, and respectful. This isn't a call to fight fire with fire, this is a call to balance the Elements and call in the rain.

Another way to make a difference is to take part in protests. I'm a big activist and have seen what works and what doesn't. To be able to shine at our brightest we must first focus on self and ground ourselves. Peaceful protest is the most effective, and just being part of such a gathering can be like working a giant spell in which the ingredients are group intent, high energy levels, and being outside in the Elements. You can attract and send out the right message by becoming a beacon of light. Focus on the final outcome, on the coming (rather then the present) circumstances. Ask any negative emotions to leave so that you can do some real work – Magick with its greatest power.

# CONTINUING
# YOUR JOURNEY

When I was growing up I didn't know how powerful our thoughts and words really are — not until I started to see the connections with what I said or thought and the events that followed.

From my senior year of high school I lived on my own, as the circumstances at home weren't healthy for me, and for a while I lived in part of an abandoned monastery. I was working in the pre-school on a lower floor, and when the pre-school owner caught on to my living situation she suggested I take a room on one of the floors above. I wasn't allowed tell anyone I was living there. There were no lights, but at least the plumbing worked.

The monastery was huge, and it was every bit as creepy as it sounds: multiple uninhabited floors with hundreds of doors; long, empty hallways; lost spirits; and a bell that rang by itself every night at about 3 or 4 a.m. But I truly felt that one day everything would turn out for the best. I had a purpose on this Earth and I was going to fulfill it. So every night I knelt on the floor and prayed to the wooden cross on a wall in my room (it hung in the only spot the Moon was able to reach, through the small window). I gave thanks for all the opportunities I was being given and for a place I could lay my head where no one could harm me, and I asserted my belief that I would continue to be blessed and guided to whatever I was meant to be.

And every day things got a little easier. I continued to align with opportunities that eventually led me to where I am now. It hasn't been a smooth ride and I've been through a lot of changes, but no matter how difficult some of my experiences, they have brought me to where I want to be, both spiritually and physically. My eyes are finally open to the truth that lives within.

Why am I sharing this story with you? Because I want you to understand the power of positive thinking even at the darkest of times. Life isn't easy, and it takes a lot of work to get where you want to be, but you have the ability and strength to get there and to manifest what you want. You have a responsibility to yourself and to the world to embrace fully who you are and to share your Magick.

The craft of Magick isn't something you just dabble in — it's a way of life. If you don't like that idea then this may not be the path for you. However, my intuition tells me that all those who have chosen to read this book and dwell in its wisdom are most definitely on the right path. We're here to shine our Magick into the universe itself, and this can only be done by those who are ready and willing to embrace the Witch within.

# A Love Letter

*Dearest Witch*

*Learning about Witchcraft can be a bit overwhelming, especially when there are thousands of books and online articles on the subject and it's hard to know which ones to trust. So I wrote this book to help you build the foundations for connecting to self, to healing, to our Magick, and to our craft.*

*You don't have to follow any book, not even this book, 100 per cent — in fact you don't have to follow any books at all. Take what you want from any lessons you learn and include the knowledge in your own practice. Just do what feels comfortable and natural to you.*

*I know many Witches who follow a certain path or type of craft. They identify as Green Witches, Kitchen Witches, Electric Witches, Sea Witches, and many others. But if you* want to follow a different path or create one of your own, then do it, dear Witches. Mold it and shape it, explore and practice, until it feels just right for you.

For those who are just starting with Witchcraft or have been doing it without their authentic selves, success can take time. There will be days when you feel lost, stuck, and overwhelmed. Be strong and, most importantly, never stop believing in yourself and in your power. With patience and practice – a lot of practice – you'll get better. You'll evolve into a fully embodied, powerful Witch, breathing Magick each and every day.

To all of the Witches struggling out there – those with broken homes or hearts, and those with nowhere to turn or no one to confide in; to any Witch who has suffered and is now rising from the ashes: I love you. I care for you and I will never stop speaking up for us all. You are worthy, and you must never forget how sacred you are. Life may hit hard, but you can hit back harder. You're stronger then you'll ever know. Use what you have, stay safe, and remember to always keep a grateful heart.

Most importantly, I'm immensely proud of you all for diving into the depths of your inner Witch. I hope that this book has given you healing, strength, and a deeper understanding of self, and that it's brought you closer to your truth and your craft. There is no end to the journey of your Magick – you'll always have new things to learn and to challenge you — so remember that you're both capable and powerful. As you continue to learn about yourself, welcome each aspect with a loving and compassionate heart. Always stay authentic, and always remember that you're Magick.

*The Witch within thanks you for embracing her.*

# Stay Connected

Community has always been, and always will be, sacred to me. Please stay connected with me through social media and sign up for the newsletters on my website. Tag me with your pictures, including any of Magickal workings from this book. You can also message me directly on my sites.

**November Sage Apothecary**
- 🌐 novembersage.com
- 📷 @novembersage
- **f** @novembersage

**November Sage Herbarium – A Witch Healers' School**
- 🌐 novembersageherbarium.com
- 📷 @novembersageherbarium
- **f** @novembersageherbarium

Wishing you a beautiful and Magickal journey ahead.

*Juliet Diaz*

# Resources

Here are a few of my favorite Magickal retailers from around the world. They offer all sorts of Witchy goods including oils, candles, and herbs. Some stores ship worldwide, but if you're a hands-on Witch or like to visit a store in person, I hope one of these will be near to you.

## USA

**November Sage Apothecary**
14 State Route 5, Palisades Park, NJ 07650
Tel: (1) 201 877 6695
info@novembersage.com
www.novembersage.com

**HausWitch Home and Healing**
144 Washington Street, Salem, MA 01970
Tel: (1) 978 594 8950
www.housewitchstore.com

## Canada
**Seven Sisters Ritual**
www.etsy.com/shop/SevenSistersRitual

# UK

**Mysteries London**
34 Shorts Gardens, London WC2H 9PX
Tel: +44 (0)20 7240 3688
london@mysteries.co.uk
www.mysteries.co.uk

**Mysteries Brighton**
54 Gardner Street, Brighton, East Sussex BN1 1UN
Tel: +44 (0)1273 690360
brighton@mysteries.co.uk
www.mysteries.co.uk

**White Witch**
1 Church St, Waltham Abbey, Essex EN9 1DX
Tel: +44 (0)1992 712794
info@witchesofwalthamabbey.co.uk
www.witchesofwalthamabbey.com

**A Coven of Witches**
The Cross, Burley, Hampshire BH24 4AA
Tel: +44 (0)1425 402449
sales@covenofwitches.co.uk
www.covenofwitches.co.uk

**The Wyrd Shop**
154 Canongate, Edinburgh EH8 8DD
Tel: +44 (0)131 557 2293
sales@wyrdshop.com
www.wyrdshop.com

**Everywitchway**
Three Ways, Back Lane, Skerne, Driffield,
    Yorkshire YO25 9HP
Tel: +44 (0)1377 241063
info@everywitchway.co.uk
www.everywitchway.co.uk

## Australia
**Spellbox**
Shop 17, Royal Arcade, 331–339 Bourke Street Mall,
    Melbourne VIC 3000
Tel: (61) 3 9639 7077
magick@spellbox.com.au
www.spellbox.com.au

# ABOUT THE AUTHOR

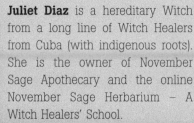

Juliet Diaz

**Juliet Diaz** is a hereditary Witch from a long line of Witch Healers from Cuba (with indigenous roots). She is the owner of November Sage Apothecary and the online November Sage Herbarium – A Witch Healers' School.

Juliet is a Healer, seer, and herbalist, and she holds a Master of Science in Herbal Medicine. She is known for her abilities as a natural healer and her gift of communicating with plants, trees, and nature spirits. Juliet was born with extrasensory abilities and signs of her natural gifts, including healing, energy reading, and communication with spirit and other realms, shone through from the age of three.

She believes that Magick lives within us all and feels passionate about bringing truth into the world and inspiring others to step into their power.

@awitchspurpose

@awitchspurpose

**www.awitchspurpose.com**

# HAY HOUSE
*Look within*

Join the conversation about latest products,
events, exclusive offers and more.

**f**  Hay House UK

🐦  @HayHouseUK

📷  @hayhouseuk

💜  healyourlife.com

*We'd love to hear from you!*